what's going on

A History of the Vietnam Era

MICHAEL HAYES

Published by:
Trine Day LLC
PO Box 577
Walterville, OR 97489
1-800-556-2012
www.TrineDay.com
trineday@icloud.com

Library of Congress Control Number: 2020937283

Hayes, Michael.
what's going on: A History of the Vietnam Era—1st ed.
p. cm.
Epub (ISBN-13) 978-1-63424-293-6
Kindle (ISBN-13) 978-1-63424-294-3
Print (ISBN-13) 978-1-63424-292-9
1. Vietnamese Conflict, 1961-1975 -- Personal narratives, American. 2. Vietnamese wars, 1961-1975. -- Personal observations - Critical studies . 3. Vietnam War, 1961-1975 -- Social aspects -- United States. 4.Soldiers -- United States -- Biography. I. Title

First Edition
10 9 8 7 6 5 4 3 2 1

Printed in the USA
Distribution to the Trade by:
Independent Publishers Group (IPG)
814 North Franklin Street
Chicago, Illinois 60610
312.337.0747
www.ipgbook.com

DEDICATED TO
NORA HAYES

"Let us begin the revolution and let us begin it with love: All of us, black, white, and gold, male and, female, have it, within our power to create a world we could bear out of the desert we inhabit for we hold our very fate in our hands."
– Kate Millet, Writer and Activist

"I wonder whether the lessons we absorbed at such tremendous cost are being passed on to future generations? If they are not understood, or if they are forgotten, are we doomed to repeat the same mistakes, commit the same crimes, repeat the same disasters, spread the same sorrows?"[1]
– Bao Ninh, Writer

CONTENTS

PROLOGUE

I'm going on a journey ... you come too. It'll be challenging but I'm certain that we can do it. I would not have asked you otherwise. This is a trip that will bring us back in time. It is a voyage to discover first hand what was going on in Vietnam and in America when we were at war with one another.

The situation was nothing if not real odd. After all, the two countries have so much in common. Both are comprised, for instance, of truly beautiful human beings that love perhaps more than anything else independence and equality. The fact that we for years made unprecedented efforts to kill one another just does not appear to make any sense. Then why did it happen? After this trip (should you decide to take it) you will have the answer to that question and to many more.

You'll also be made mindful of how you and your companions are not the first people to regularly face very serious problems, frequently involving life and death. For instance, 11,000 American teenagers died in Vietnam. How did the generation of the Vietnam Era meet with the serious issues of their day? In addition to war they dealt with a lot of the other tests that you have been witness to: sexism, racism, bigotry towards the LGBTQ community and extreme violence. Some of their efforts succeeded in changing things for the better and others met with grave disappointment. But much can be learned from both outcomes.

Our trip (hopefully by now you've decided to come along) is going to take place at five Landing Zones (LZ's). First, a whirlwind trip through Vietnam's past. Second, the stories of the main people who led the American war effort. Third, the culture of the era. Fourth, the true stories of the young women and men who were of the time. Fifth, you'll discover how those same people feel today.

This trip isn't going to provide the solution to all of your challenges but it will, at last, give you some direction as you take your turn and change the world.

And now the time has arrived. The rotor blades are spinning faster and faster as the engine revs on the especially equipped helicopter. The dust rises and the chopper is ready to lift off.

I'm going on a journey ... you come too.

LZ ALPHA

AN INTRODUCTION

"It was patriotism, not communism, that inspired me."[2]

Ho Chi Minh held America in high esteem, once. He appreciated the cool styles of Brooklyn and Harlem and the revolutionary history of Boston. Ho idolized George Washington and the way he led a war for freedom. He thought highly of Thomas Jefferson, The Declaration of Independence and, in particular, the idea that everyone is created equal. He admired Abraham Lincoln for helping to bring about an end to slavery and reunifying the North with the South.[3] He thought that the fact that as upstart colonies we had beaten the heck out of an imperialist super power and sent them back to Europe was nothing short of terrific.

Ho appreciated that the United States never attempted a land grab in Asia and he thought Franklin Roosevelt was great because he called for an end to colonization around the world[4] [5]including in Viet Nam[6] and resolved to award independence to the Philippines following the end of World War II.[7] [8]Ho dreamed that America would openly support his own efforts to secure independence for his fledgling Democratic Republic of Vietnam. For above all else Ho was a patriot and yearned for the freedom that other nations, like the US, sometimes take for granted.

His beloved Vietnam had a civilization dating back at least six thousand years when the people resided in hamlets, cultivated rice and occupied houses built on stilts to defend against floods and the occasional ravenous tiger. Then for a millennium the Vietnamese were under the control of the Chinese until, after much struggle, they were finally driven out in 938(ce).[9] In the 17th Century the French sent Catholic missionaries to the region[10] and, later, soldiers to "protect" those who had converted,[11] a tactic that they implemented successfully in subjugating others, including for example, some indigenous North Americans. By the late 19th Century France had successfully colonized the region, which included not only Vietnam but also neighboring Laos and Cambodia and christened it "French Indochina."[12]

They ruled through Emperors and French speaking Vietnamese officials known as Mandarins who, as puppets, carried out France's every command. The Vietnamese people, for the most part, were relegated to third class citizenship in their own homeland.[13] The French formed large rubber plantations and pushed opium[14] [15] while setting out to construct a Vietnam in their own image. Most of the occupying French didn't even bother to learn the language. As one can easily imagine many Vietnamese grew to despise their imperialist masters.

Ho's father was a Mandarin and as such Ho was raised in a relatively privileged setting.[16] While in high school he learned his country's history and combined with his own observations came to the realization that France was the enemy of Vietnam. The recognition of this fact led to his being expelled as he began to speak out and soon caught the attention of the French Officials' judgmental eyes. Many young people were imprisoned for less than Ho's behavior and he, therefore, quite naturally thought it prudent to skip out of Vietnam before he too ended up in a penitentiary.[17]

And so at the age of 20, in 1911, he was gone and would not return for thirty years when he was ready to lead a revolution that would ultimately drive France completely out of South East Asia.[18] He worked on ships that eventually brought him to the United States where he was employed in menial positions. Later, he traveled to England and then to France where he learned about Socialism and was active in the party. It wasn't long before he became discouraged by his French comrades' preoccupation with trying to change domestic policies and almost not at all with the issues that Indochina faced.

With the conclusion of World War I Ho's expectations were raised when President Woodrow Wilson proclaimed that the interests of colonial people should be given equal weight with those of their rulers.[19] Ho showed up at Versailles where the peace treaty was being crafted and, donned in a rented suit in an effort to comport a distinguished air, the gaunt young man audaciously presented a petition asking for greater freedom for the people of Vietnam.[20] To his disappointment, and contributing to his disillusionment, the petition was completely ignored.[21]

Eventually, he traveled to Russia where he hung his hopes on the new Communist regime that vigorously supported anti-colonialism.[22] Although embracing Communist philosophy, Ho was far more interested in independence[23] and so was not exactly favored by the big shots in Moscow who wanted French Communists to manage Indochinese affairs anyway. Nevertheless, he managed to ultimately be dispatched to China where he eventually formed the Communist Party of Indochina (CPI).[24][25][26]

By 1940 he was an established leader as well as a sophisticated world traveler capable of speaking English, French, Vietnamese, Chinese and Russian.[27] He had developed a profound understanding of communist philosophy and helped spread the ideology throughout Indochina and other parts of Asia.[28] Described as sensitive, gentle and frail Ho did not give the appearance of someone who could lead a violent and ruthless revolution yet that is exactly what he was prepared to do. When World War II broke out and the Japanese wrested control of Vietnam from the French Ho saw an opportunity to return to his homeland and take advantage of the confusion caused by the change in regimes. And so in February of 1941 he was back in Vietnam for the first time in three decades.[29]

Ho and his band of just 34 revolutionaries, including three women, formed the Vietnam Independence League better known as The Viet Minh.[30] They planned resistance to the Japanese occupying force, passed intelligence to America's CIA forerunner the Office of Strategic Services (OSS) on troop movements and helped, at great risk, to rescue downed US pilots.[31][32] Ho asked the United States for assistance and President Franklin Roosevelt responded by sending a cadre of OSS agents to arm and train Ho's rapidly growing corps. He enthusiastically welcomed them and, indeed, was honored and encouraged by the Americans' presence.[33]

[34]Meanwhile, a terrific famine took the lives of more than one million Vietnamese while French and Japanese officials did nothing to provide relief.[35] The Viet Minh on the other hand broke open granaries and distributed rice to the people. Rice that the imperialists had been hoarding for themselves.[36]

When the Japanese were finally defeated in 1945 Ho and his followers, now grown into a large army, marched, with great fanfare, into the capital city of Hanoi and declared the establishment of the Democratic Republic of Vietnam. The local people, still stinging from the neglect during the famine, plastered the city with posters decrying French colonialism and declaring, "Long Live Vietnamese Independence" and "Long live the USSR and the USA."[37] Ho stood on a platform in front of hundreds of thousands of his fellow countrymen and read his Declaration of Vietnamese Independence that began as homage to the United States, "All men are created equal. They are endowed by their creator with certain inalienable rights; among these are life, liberty and the pursuit of happiness."[38]

Then the rumble of a plane's engine could be heard above the crowd. A hush fell over the great mass of people as everyone turned their eyes upward in nervous anticipation wondering just who this was. When the plane flew lower the flag, painted on the aircraft, of the United States of America could be discerned and with that a cheer began and spread through the crowd like a wave until it became a magnificent roar.[39]

But their elation was short lived because the French soon marched back in to reclaim their colony. Ho warned the occupiers, "You can kill 10 of my men for every one I kill of yours, yet even at those odds, you will lose and I will win."[40] As war broke out with France Ho turned once again to the United States for support but, alas, Roosevelt was dead.[41] The new President, Harry Truman, was more concerned with keeping France happy in the hope that they wouldn't ally themselves with Russia than he was with ending colonialism. America, therefore, provided France with financial backing, arms (including a jellied petroleum that bursts into flame on impact called napalm[42]) and a handful of military advisors.

The Cold War between the US and Russia was of central concern to Truman.[43] He didn't want to see Russia or China, for that matter, gain even a single inch of territory. He failed to comprehend that neither of those countries had very much interest in Vietnam.[44] Russia's leader Josef Stalin was particularly preoccupied with European expansion.[45] China, was distracted with a budding Korean War, and was reluctant to get too deeply involved in yet another conflict. Ho Chi Minh and the Vietnamese people had exactly zero interest in becoming a puppet of any other country inasmuch as independence and patriotic pride were deeply ingrained in their hearts.[46]

Later, as Vietnam and France fought on, President Truman's successor Dwight D. Eisenhower continued to support France, providing billions of dollars, covering 80% of their budget,[47] [48]to hold on to the colonies. In addition, he deployed hundreds more advisors to Indochina. Eisenhower argued that it was essential to keep western/capitalist control over the region lest the rest of South East Asia follow Vietnam and fall, as would a "row of dominoes," into Communist hands.[49] [50]

For seven long years a brutal war raged between Vietnam and France. Under the able leadership of Vietnamese General Vo Nguyen Giap, a decisive battle at Dienbienphu (d-n, b-n, foo)[51] helped force the French to agree to divide the nation in two, North and South, and recognize absolute independence in the North. At this point the US decided that they would do everything they could to keep the Communist regime of the North from gaining any more territory.

Pro-Ho Chi Minh Vietnamese headed north and pro-Western Vietnamese as well as many Catholics foreseeing serious Communist oppression moved south mostly on US naval vessels. However, several thousand Viet Minh surreptitiously stayed in the South and would form the nucleus of guerrillas that became known as the National Liberation Front (NLF) but perhaps more famously as the Vietcong (VC).

The North was now under the leadership of Ho and the South under a chubby little autocrat by the name of Ngo Dinh Diem (d-m), whom the US mistakenly[52] hoped would serve as their faithful puppet. According to the peace agreement after two years elections were scheduled to be held and the winner would rule over a reunited nation.[53] Eisenhower took note of the fact that polls indicated Ho would defeat Diem handsomely[54] and, therefore, the US and Diem blocked efforts to conduct the election and, indeed, it was never held.[55]

Resistance to Diem was met with swift and harsh retaliation. In addition, his cruel and apparently aloof attitude soon created a chasm between himself and his own people. Meanwhile, Ho was preoccupied with rebuilding the North, which had been devastated by the long war with France. He offered little support for the fast-growing resistance in the South in part because he didn't want to give the US an excuse for further interference.[56] However, a more aggressive member of the Northern leadership by the name of Le Duan stepped up and used his authority to begin to send soldiers and supplies south to help overthrow Diem and reunify Vietnam.[57] Although active in the prosecution of the war the now venerable Uncle Ho, as he became known, became a beloved figurehead but the main effort for reunification of the country fell to more ambitious, often ruthless and determined youth.[58]

By now the US government's leaders had made a firm decision to take a stand against communism in Vietnam. Hundreds of millions of dollars were sent to prop up the divisive and largely unpopular Diem regime. By 1960 there were about 1,500 American, largely noncombatant, advisors in Vietnam when a new President came to the White House and the fate of America's relationship with the small South East Asian country would be placed squarely upon his shoulders.

Endnotes

1   Geoffrey C. Ward and Ken Burns, *The Vietnam War: An Intimate History* (New York, New York: Alfred A. Knopf, 2017), 463. (Henceforth TVW)

2   Stanley Karnow, "Ho Chi Minh; He married nationalism to communism and perfected the deadly art of guerrilla warfare," *Time,* April 13, 1998. content.time.com (Henceforth HCM)

3   Fredrik Logevall, *Embers of War: The Fall of an Empire and the Making of America's Vietnam* (New York, N.Y.: Random House, 2012) 11. (Henceforth EOW)

4   *IBID*, 46.

5   Hugh Boyle, Author's Interview, March 3, 2018. (Henceforth AI)

6   Franklin Roosevelt memo to Secretary of State Cordell Hull, "Indo China should not go back to France." January 24, 1944. National Archives, Washington, D.C.

7   Larry H. Addington, *America's War in Vietnam: A Short Narrative History* (Bloomington, Indiana: Indiana University Press, 2000), 30. (Henceforth AWV)

8   EOW, 48.

9   Max Hastings, *Vietnam: An Epic Tragedy, 1945-1975* (New York, N.Y.: Harper, 2018), 2. (Henceforth VAET)

10   AWV, 6.

11   *IBID*, 8.

12   *IBID*, 10.

13   Ha Van Thu and Tran Hong Duc, *A Brief Chronology of Vietnamese History* (Hanoi, Vietnam: The Gioi Publishers, 2014) 148.

14   VAET, 2.

15   AWV, 12.

16   Christopher Goscha, *Vietnam: A New History* (New York, N.Y.: Basic Books, 2016) 137-138. (Henceforth VANH)

17   VAET, 5.

18   AWV, 15.

19   Boyle, AI.

20   VANH, 139.

21   AWV, 16.

22   VANH, 141.

23   *IBID*, 5.

24   AWV, 18.

25   Fredrik Logevall, AI, March 28, 2018.

26   VANH, 144.

27   VAET, 6.

28   VANH, 144.

29   *IBID*, 194.

30   VAET, 11.

31   AWV, 25.

32   VANH, 196.

33   AWV, 26.

34   VANH, 197.

35   Howard Zinn, *A People's History of the United States*. (New York, N.Y.: Harper and Row, 1980) 461. (Henceforth APH)

36   VANH, 199.

37   *IBID*, 182.

38   APH, 460.

39   AWV, 28.

40   HCM, 1.

41   Ho Chi Minh letter to Harry S. Truman, *"I therefore most earnestly appeal to you personally and to the American people to interfere urgently in support of our independence."* February 28, 1946. National Archives, Washington, D.C.

42   EOW 267.

43   *IBID*, 196.

44   *IBID*, 225.

45   Boyle, AI.

46   AWV, 36.

47   *IBID*, 39.

48   Boyle, AI.

49   VANH, 282.

50   Boyle, AI.

51   AWV, 42.

52   VANH, 313.

53   APH, 463.

54   IBID, 463.

55   EOW, 651–652.

56   Logevall, AI.

57   AWV, 52.

58   VANH, 319-320.

MAKING WAR

"He hadn't yet made up his mind."

This early morning was as pitch black as the sea upon which his boat was afloat as 2:30 neared. Suddenly and seemingly out of nowhere, a Japanese destroyer came steaming in, fast and hard. When it smashed into the side of the vessel he thought, "This is how it feels to be killed." But he was not killed while he watched as half of his PT109 began to sink 1,200 feet to the bottom of the Pacific Ocean. He did not die when the sea around him became engulfed in red, yellow and blue flames as the gasoline that spilled from his bisected boat blazed away.

Two of the crew died in the collision. The ten survivors dutifully followed their skipper who was now being tested, as never before. Swimming in the warm and barracuda infested Pacific waters on August 2, 1943 young Lieutenant (jg) John Fitzgerald Kennedy was in the process of discovering of what he was truly made.[1] He led his crew to a deserted

Island where they managed to elude deadly enemy patrols for days until they were, at last, rescued. Kennedy was awarded medals and lauded as a hero[2] and after the public learned the story of that unforgettable adventure his political career was launched and his historically quick journey to the White House and its Oval Office was underway.

JFK, as he was popularly known, was well liked, smart, wealthy and associated with many very important people. He was a Harvard graduate and greatly valued other well-educated and highly intelligent people.[3] During his meteoric rise to power his interest rested largely in international affairs. Indeed, when he took the oath of office as America's youngest elected President his entire Inaugural Address focused on foreign policy.

Early in his Administration his top military men poorly advised him regarding a failed invasion of Cuba and for that reason he did not strongly rely on them when making his most important military decisions. He depended far more on his Secretary of Defense, Robert McNamara as well as his younger brother, Bobby, who served as Attorney General, and a handful of others.

JFK supported Diem because he thought that the hardline ruler stood the best chance of achieving a somewhat democratic nation that was cooperative with the US. He responded to Diem's requests for more and more support by providing more money, more weapons and more advisors. The goal was to get the South Vietnamese to be able to defend themselves against Northern forces and the VC without a major US military involvement. With this aim in mind Kennedy advanced the Special Forces, adding the Green Beret to their uniform as "a symbol of excellence, a badge of courage, a mark of distinction in the fight for freedom."[4] These highly trained Army soldiers would serve as advisors and equip the Vietnamese to eventually fight the war on their own.

However, as time went on the advisors began to become frustrated with the fighting ability and spirit that many in the Army of South Vietnam clearly lacked. The Americans started to join in on the combat themselves and, naturally, the casualty list began to slowly creep upward. All of these developments were downplayed to the American people.[5]

Meanwhile, JFK helped with the negotiations of a peace treaty in neighboring Laos[6] by forming a coalition government between US-friendly leaders and Communist forces. The Laotian Communists were granted control of an eastern portion of the country, which was an area that bordered North and South Vietnam and made it easier for the Army of North Vietnam (NVA) to transport troops and supplies to the South via a network of roads known as the Ho Chi Minh Trail.[7]

Because he was worried about the developing quagmire, JFK became guilty of misleading the public by minimizing America's swiftly growing role in the war. For instance, in an interview with the TV anchorman Walter Cronkite he claimed that 47 soldiers had been killed when 134 had actually died up to that point in his Administration.[8] He approved the "dispatch of agents to North Vietnam" to engage in "sabotage and light harassment."[9] He also raised the stakes by authorizing the use of the deadly toxin Agent Orange[10] and continued the use of the burning gel napalm. As time went on Kennedy grew increasingly frustrated with the situation. Vietnam was already beginning to smell like a real loser. The entire North was permanently under communist rule; many Buddhists in the South despised Diem because he oppressed them while strongly favoring the minority Catholics and the VC controlled large portions of the rural South. Diem grew increasingly unpopular and when an elderly Buddhist monk self-immolated in protest Kennedy was badly shaken. High-ranking South Vietnamese military officials were secretly expressing their desire to overthrow Diem and hoped to offer a more unifying style of government. JFK's advisors were split on the subject but those who favored the plot worked feverishly to gain Kennedy's support. Finally, with US approval, the coup went ahead in early November of 1963.[11] Diem was taken prisoner and summarily executed.[12]

When JFK learned the news of Diem's murder he blanched and rushed from the room. What had he done? Was Diem's blood now on his hands? He had hoped perhaps that the autocrat would take up an offer by the US to leave Vietnam; however, he would have been naive to think that Diem's power-hungry adversaries would not have murdered him before he was able to make his getaway.[13]

Now what? Some mess! 16,000 Americans were stationed in Vietnam, hundreds and hundreds of millions of taxpayers' dollars had been spent and scores of American soldiers had been killed. The new governments were comprised of a series of inept and corrupt generals who did not possess the ability to unify the country. Meanwhile, the communists were encouraged by the overthrow of the much-despised Diem. At this point America would either have to make a much stronger commitment to a lost cause or embrace a strategy for withdrawal.

Tragically, just a few short weeks after the Diem assassination JFK was shot dead while riding in a motorcade in Dallas, Texas. No one knows and may never know for certain what he would have done regarding Vietnam had he not been gunned down. Robert McNamara later said that he believed

JFK, after his likely re-election in 1964, would have recalled American troops from Vietnam and left the fighting to the South Vietnamese. Bobby Kennedy believed his brother would have negotiated a coalition government as had been done in Laos,[14] thereby providing a way to declare victory and then go home.[15] President Kennedy's National Security Advisor McGeorge Bundy said what is probably correct, "He hadn't yet made up his mind."[16]

On the day JFK died all of North Vietnam was under communist control while the Republic of Vietnam controlled less than half of the south.[17] The truth is that the war was already unwinnable and America's role had barely just begun. 171 Americans were killed to date and there were another 58,000 plus waiting, unsuspectingly, to meet the same fate. 58,000 plus.

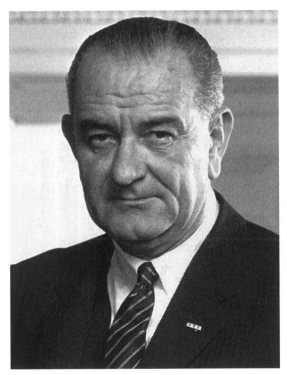

"… like grandma's nightshirt – it covered everything."

Vice President Lyndon Baines Johnson was an ambitious career politician who ascended to the Presidency following JFK's assassination. LBJ, as he was known, was not happy about how he finally ended up in the Oval Office because he saw himself as an "accidental" President and so more than anything else he not only wanted to be but also believed that he absolutely needed to be elected in his own right.

Although Johnson was an extremely able politician he harbored a strong sense of insecurity along with a fear of failure and a bottomless need to be loved. His style stood in sharp contrast to that of JFK's. Kennedy was comfortable being around highly educated and accomplished people while LBJ felt inferior in their presence. And unlike JFK and many of his staff, whom Johnson kept on, he had not been educated in an Ivy League University such as Harvard or Yale but rather at the provincial Southwest Texas Teachers College. Also, unlike his predecessor, he was not a handsome man, he was raised in poverty and did not emerge from WWII as a colorful hero. Where JFK was cool and gracious LBJ could be crude and vulgar.[18] For example, he would sometimes sit on the toilet bowl with the door open while he led political discussions with his disgusted and uncomfortable staff.[19]

However, LBJ knew possibly more than anyone else of his time, including his predecessor, how to get things done in Washington and he was determined to realize his dream of completing what his idol Franklin D. Roosevelt had started with the New Deal. He wanted to transform America into a "Great Society." He envisioned eliminating all poverty, discrimination and ignorance throughout the United States. But in order to achieve his monumental ambitions he would need time, lots of time. First, he would have to win the election in '64 and get a full four years of his own. His opponent was Republican Barry Goldwater, whom LBJ portrayed as unstable and, therefore, far too dangerous to be allowed to be Commander-in-Chief in control of the United States' incredible arsenal of nuclear weapons.

On the other hand, he portrayed himself as the peace candidate. Goldwater claimed that Johnson would be too passive to stop communist expansion around the world and afraid to use military power. LBJ realized that he would have to strike a delicate balance between being tough on America's enemies yet not unduly militaristic.

When an American destroyer, the USS *Maddox*, was fired upon in the Gulf of Tonkin off the coast of North Vietnam LBJ used the incident to serve two purposes.[20] One, he would show that he was not afraid to use force by ordering, in retaliation, a limited bombing of some military targets in North Vietnam. Second, he could gain the approval of Congress to take strong action in the future by overseeing the passage of the Gulf of Tonkin Resolution.[21]

Congress passed the resolution with only two nay votes and thereby gave the President almost unlimited authority to wage a war on Vietnam.

As Johnson put it, "...like grandma's nightshirt – it covered everything."[22] He would not use this authority, however, right away. He would bide his time until after he secured his essential election victory.[23] Unlike JFK he was not all that interested in foreign affairs because he was anxious to get his Great Society reforms underway. He wanted to quickly solve the problem of Vietnam, which he saw as an annoyance and distraction from the really important things that he yearned to accomplish.

He would give his military whatever they needed to bring the Vietnam conflict to a swift conclusion. But at the same time he had to be very careful. By now China and the Soviet Union changed their policy and were wholeheartedly supporting North Vietnam's efforts.

"Hey, Hey, LBJ, how many kids did you kill today?"

When LBJ awoke on the morning of Wednesday November 4th, 1964 he might have had to remind himself that it was not all just one big beautiful dream. He had won! He was no longer the "accidental" President because he buried his opponent with a landslide victory. He amassed nearly 62% of the vote, gathered almost 16 million more popular votes than did Goldwater and won in the Electoral College 486 to 52. Any way you looked at it he was unquestionably the big winner.[24] Johnson believed that with every vote cast in his favor the American people were telling him that he was loved. Now he had the mandate that he so desperately wanted and the confidence he required to build his Great Society and thereby become the most successful American President ever![25]

Yet, he had one thing in particular that he had to deal with that he would rather have not had on his plate; a small thorn in his side called The Republic of South Vietnam, 9,000 miles from his Oval Office. It was a country where, following Diem's murder, one group of corrupt military incompetents after the next took control of the reins of government. He had his reasons for not simply ending America's involvement in Vietnam. He believed he could not walk away from his commitment to stand up to communist aggression around the world. Americans had already shed their blood in Vietnam and a fortune had been spent in propping up the governments. The South Vietnamese couldn't hold their country together alone, of that he was quite certain, and there was also a matter of American pride and its global prestige.

Johnson had many supporters that wanted nothing more than to flex their military muscles around the world because there was money to be made, power and authority to be gained in the conduct of this war. LBJ decided to commit to the fray while already knowing it was a lost cause. Still, this was the United States of America, the most powerful country in the history of humankind with a stupendous military force and unlimited resources at its disposal. How could it be possible that we would not win in the end? From the outset LBJ opted to embrace denial.

As if entering into a cold swimming pool, he did not dive into the deep part but first gingerly dipped a toe in the shallow end. He would respond to North Vietnamese attacks by strategically bombing very carefully chosen sites. As the months passed he saw that that was not having enough of an impact and so he stepped up the bombing and expanded it into neighboring Laos in an effort to halt or at least to curtail the movement of enemy forces steadily streaming down the Ho Chi Minh Trail.[26]

As did his predecessor he chose not to tell the American people the whole truth. He downplayed his actions in order to keep the focus on his Great Society programs and to not appear as a hypocrite after having been elected as the peace candidate. He feared that if the American people knew what was going on they might begin to protest. It turned out that he was right. As intrepid war correspondents reported to America about the true conduct of the conflict[27] some people began to show up in front of the White House windows. Inside, Johnson could hear their taunting chants. At first only a handful appeared, later it was hundreds, thousands, tens of thousands and finally hundreds of thousands with their incessant chant, "Hey, Hey, LBJ, how many kids did you kill today?"

But that was not yet. For now he basked in the glory of his victory and imagined all of the great things he would accomplish. In the meantime, in Vietnam, the Vietcong began to attack the airfields where the Americans housed their planes. The man that LBJ had put in charge of military operations, General William Westmoreland, requested 3,500 soldiers to provide security. The President agreed and in March of 1965, without the permission or even the knowledge of the South Vietnamese government and utilizing the authority granted to him under the Gulf of Tonkin Resolution, the first official American combat troops set foot on Vietnamese soil.[28] They were there not to advise or support the South Vietnamese Army but rather to fight the VC and the NVA personally. This was the first solid indication that it would soon become America's war.[29]

Initially, the soldiers defended the perimeter of the airfield but when attacked with mortars they ventured further out to find the source. When they were hit by artillery fire they moved out even further and before long they were fighting and dying far away from the airfields. Westmorland then asked for more troops in order to cover the larger territory and Johnson dutifully agreed. A pattern developed whereby Johnson would send soldiers and for a brief while Westmorland would be satisfied but then he'd ask for more and Johnson would send them and the whole process would be repeated again and again and again.

Soon the United States had indeed taken over the responsibility for the conduct of the conflict and American causalities began to mount; 50, 100, 500, a thousand, two thousand and more killed in action. Now the war took on a new meaning. It was no longer about just stopping the spread of communism but instead to not let the soldiers who were killed have died in vain. LBJ believed we were left with no choice but to stay.

NVA kept pouring in from down the Ho Chi Minh Trail. The VC grew in numbers and controlled more of the rural areas of South Vietnam. They were willing to take as much punishment as the US could dish out for as long as it took to gain reunification and independence.

How to win under these troubling circumstances? A big problem that LBJ faced was that this war was not like World War II, for instance, where the enemy was a clearly defined entity. The Vietcong generally did not wear uniforms, they were not all young men and they did not fight with the largely conventional methods utilized by, say, the Nazis. The enemy could easily be a young girl or boy living in a poverty-stricken section of the capital, Saigon, for instance. LBJ could not simply allow the bombing of certain suspect neighborhoods in large cities in the South or declare the neighborhood a "free fire zone" where soldiers were authorized to kill anything that moved. These, after all, were the very same people, neighborhoods and cities America was there to protect and preserve.

Even if Johnson used his unlimited authority to order every soldier to stand shoulder to shoulder and march from the southern most tip of Vietnam all the way to the Chinese border in the north and kill every man, woman and child that crossed their path the VC and the NVA could easily slip into their neighboring countries to orchestrate counter-attacks to the rear. What then? Would we openly and unlimitedly invade Cambodia and Laos too? Would we chase the Vietnamese westward and thereby create new enemies, new wars, in these neighboring countries?

From where would the additional soldiers required to wage such a war come? An already unpopular method of forcing military service on young people, the Draft, would have to be expanded. There would have to be fewer exemptions and so the clever could no longer find refuge on college campuses, rich young men could not easily bribe doctors and receive a dispensation for fake health problems, those who sought refuge in the National Guard or the Reserves would no longer be protected from having to have to go to the war because they too would be called in for the fight. Additionally, there was already a burgeoning "stop the war" movement and a demand for perhaps hundreds of thousands more soldiers would only add fuel to the antiwar movement's fire and further divide the nation.

If American soldiers approached the Chinese border what would prevent China from wholeheartedly entering the war? They were already sending hundreds of thousands of troops into North Vietnam to perform noncombat duties in order to free up NVA soldiers to march southward.[30] What would keep them from sending hundreds of thousands more or even a million troops across the border, armed to the teeth and eager to fight, as they did in Korea?[31] [32] And if they did would we then be compelled to invade China as well?

And what about Russia? Their ships heavily laden with ordnance and other supplies were constantly steaming in and out of North Vietnamese ports. What if we intentionally sank their vessels resulting in the death of scores of Russian sailors? The Soviets would quite naturally be expected to retaliate and perhaps initiate another war and even a nuclear exchange. Was Vietnam worth starting World War III over? If LBJ decided to use a nuclear bomb against North Vietnam what would stop Russia or China from providing the North with a nuclear bomb or two to drop on strategic locations in the South?

In denial, LBJ hung his slim and unrealistic hopes on the claims of General Westmoreland and his promises of impending victory. Westmoreland believed that if Americans killed enough of the enemy eventually they would no longer be able to offer meaningful resistance. He fought a war of attrition and demanded a "body count." The number of enemy corpses amassed would determine whether or not we were winning. Problematically, the number killed was routinely and greatly exaggerated in order to please high-ranking officials and placate the American public who were anxious for any positive news.[33]

Westmoreland underestimated his enemies' resolve apparently not learning from a history that demonstrated that the Vietnamese were willing to resist the Chinese for 1,000 years before achieving victory. Surely they would be willing to resist Americans for a mere twenty or even thirty years. Evidently he forgot that they had absorbed huge losses in their war with the French before compelling them to leave. Or perhaps he too was simply deluding himself and did not want to acknowledge the inevitability of defeat.

In fact, by the spring of 1967 after two full years of heavy combat on the ground and from the air Westmoreland returned to the United States to report to Congress that indeed we were winning the war and that before much longer it would all be over. Victory was now within our grasp! The US Ambassador Ellsworth Bunker echoed Westmoreland's sentiments saying that he could "see the light at the end of the tunnel."[34] Many Americans began to rally around the cause. By now there were nearly 500,000 US troops in Vietnam and by the end of the year a total of more than 20,000 American soldiers died.

"I shall not seek, and I will not accept, the nomination of my party for another term as your President."

As 1968 dawned LBJ sat behind his desk in the Oval Office. He had at long last some reason to feel upbeat. Polls indicated that a majority of the American people supported his leadership regarding Vietnam; Westmorland reported that he had turned the corner, that his troops had killed enough of the enemy and that they would no longer be able to offer effective resistance. The war would soon be over or at least could be toned down and Johnson could devote all of his attention to what he really cared about, his war on poverty and the further advancement of Civil Rights. Vietnam had siphoned too much money away from his efforts and ate up way too much of his precious time.

He did, however, harbor serious doubts. His Secretary of Defense, Robert McNamara, had had enough and he was now ready to resign. In addition, LBJ had to know that the body-count figures were greatly exaggerated. He had to have learned by now that conventional methods of determining the outcome of this war did not apply. Yet, he could indulge in wishful thinking. Saying that we were winning, perhaps, would help to make it a reality. But it would not be long before all of his hopes were completely dashed.

Westmoreland had sent 6,000 Marines, as bait, north to Khe Sanh (kay-san) near the Demilitarized Zone (DMZ) and the border with Laos in the hope of drawing out a large number of VC and NVA in this relatively unpopulated area so that he could inflict massive casualties by artillery and airpower without many civilians caught in the fray. It wasn't long before his wish was granted and Khe Sanh was completely surrounded by more than 20,000 enemy troops.[35]

In addition, there had been intelligence reports indicating that a massive coordinated attack was about to take place. Large numbers of VC and

NVA had secretly positioned themselves in and around cities all over South Vietnam. The North Vietnamese generals had taken a page from our own George Washington's book when he surprised the British Army by crossing the Delaware River and attacking on Christmas morning in 1776. Similarly the NVA and VC would attack on the national holiday known as Tet.

80,000 enemy soldiers, almost simultaneously, attacked 36 Provincial capitals and another 64 towns and cities. After fierce fighting over the coming weeks the American and South Vietnamese armies were able to kill or capture the majority of enemy combatants including many thousands around Khe Sanh alone. At first the Tet Offensive was considered a military defeat for the NVA and the VC but the American people had trouble understanding; if we were on the verge of victory how could they have pulled off such a stunning attack?[36] Could it be that the assurances of victory were merely more empty promises? More lies?

To add to the problem General Westmoreland indicated that completing the VC's defeat would necessitate another 200,000 American service members and require an activation of the Reserves.[37] Westmoreland had already begun a plan to move nuclear weapons to Vietnam for potential use against the NVA in Khe Sanh. A flabbergasted Johnson quickly squelched that scheme.[38] [39]

Now even LBJ's biggest supporters were having their doubts. The American people questioned why, if the enemy were on the run, did American soldiers continue to die by the hundreds and thousands. In February Robert McNamara, publically choking back tears, finally quit in frustration. Senator Eugene McCarthy of Minnesota and now Senator Robert Kennedy of New York were presenting a serious challenge to LBJ for the nomination by the Democratic Party for President.

Vietnam had dashed his dreams for a Great Society. Yes, he could point to accomplishments in Civil Rights, health care and education, but his preoccupation with Vietnam and the draining of the national treasury left him far short of his hope of completely transforming the country for the good. And so it was a broken LBJ who, on March 31, 1968 appeared, somber and sober, on national television and spoke of his desire for peace in Vietnam and his willingness to negotiate an end to the war. In his conclusion LBJ shocked the nation when he said;

> *With America's sons in the fields far away, with America's future under*
> *challenge right here at home, with our hopes and the world's hopes for*
> *peace in the balance every day, I do not believe that I should devote*

*an hour or a day of my time to any personal partisan causes or to any
duties other than the awesome duties of this office--the Presidency of
your country. Accordingly, I shall not seek, and I will not accept, the
nomination of my party for another term as your President.*[40]

Vietnam brought an end to his Presidency and would forever mar his
legacy. That night he announced that he would halt much of the bombing
of North Vietnam and in exchange asked that negotiations for peace be
initiated. The leadership in Hanoi, convinced that LBJ was sincere, agreed
to talk. In June Westmoreland was relieved of his duties in Vietnam and
replaced by General Creighton Abrams. Abrams gave up on the idea of
victory over North Vietnam and instead focused on what JFK had originally hoped to do, hand the fighting over to the South Vietnamese.

"Any other way to monkey wrench it?"

Richard Nixon, known as Dick, was raised in fairly humble surroundings. Sure his father eked out a living as a grocer but it was always a
struggle and Dick and his brothers were compelled to work in the store
just to help to make ends meet. His deeply religious Quaker mother, whom
Dick with his very low bar for canonization would deem to be a saint,[41]
tried to instill important ethics such as honesty in her intelligent and hard
working boy. Yet, she could never say the words that Dick yearned most

to hear, "I love you."[42] Perhaps it was his mother's unresponsiveness to his desire to be highly valued that contributed to a deep darkness in his personality, which would many years later result in his disgracing the office that he most coveted, that of the Presidency.

A bright young man, Dick had been accepted to Harvard University and was even awarded an academic scholarship but there was no money for his transportation expenses or for his room and board and so he had to stay at home and attend a small local college called Whittier. Nixon harbored a self-destructive envy of more fortunate people and would always resent those whom he thought had things just handed to them. He carried that resentment with him for his entire life.

Following graduation near the top of his class he received a full scholarship from Duke Law School where he applied himself and again finished among the very best. During World War II he served in the Navy in the Pacific and during his free time was able to lure fellow officers, using the promise of beer and steaks as bait, into poker games and then manage to fleece his comrades of thousands of dollars.[43][44]

Following his stint in the Navy Nixon, wanting to further serve his country and to satisfy an ambitious drive, entered into politics. Dick, by nature, was introverted and socially awkward, obviously difficult traits for someone in politics where it was so important to physically connect with voters and speak publically – often extemporaneously. He did what was needed but it was extremely uncomfortable for him and frequently his discomfort would show. A Nixon performance, for instance, might include much sweating from above his upper lip while his eyes darted nervously from left to right.

Despite his obvious problems his rise in the political world was swift. First, Congressional Representative, then Senator, Vice President, then Presidential nominee for the Republican Party. His advancement was due in large part to his capitalizing on the fears of the American public regarding communism. He smeared innocent opponents and relentlessly pursued citizens that he suspected of having had ties to the Communist Party. He lost a very close race to his personable contemporary JFK, which further deepened his hatred of those far more fortunate than he. Two years later he was once again defeated when he ran for Governor of California. It appeared that Dick was finished politically until 1968 when he re-emerged as would a Phoenix rising from his own ashes to become the Republican Party's best hope to win the White House; promising to heal a nation divided by Vietnam and to bring the war to an honorable conclusion.

In June Bobby Kennedy was assassinated and before long McCarthy was brushed aside by the political establishment to clear the way for Hubert Humphrey, LBJ's Vice President, who then emerged as Nixon's opponent. At first Humphrey took a hard line on Vietnam but finally said that if he were elected he would stop all bombing of North Vietnam. As Humphrey's poll numbers rose Nixon began to fret over the prospect of facing yet another humiliating defeat.

The North Vietnamese and the Vietcong had agreed to LBJ's offer and announced that they would come to the negotiating table. The President of South Vietnam Nguyen Van Thieu (Too) was expected to participate as well. Johnson's efforts to achieve peace and Humphrey's support for the talks resulted in more good polling news for the Democrat. To stop the momentum Nixon ordered that a "monkey wrench" be thrown into the process.[45] It was arranged for one of his emissaries to meet with Thieu and promise him that if he waited until after the election to enter into the peace talks Nixon would negotiate better terms for him than would Johnson and Humphrey.

Thieu agreed and the peace talks were immediately stalled, as was Humphrey's upward trend.[46] Privately LBJ learned from his spies what Nixon had been up to and he was livid. "We could stop the killing out there," a frustrated Johnson groused, "...they're killing four or five hundred a day waiting on Nixon." When confronted by the President with the accusation Dick lied and said he would never do anything like that.[47] [48]And so by colluding with a foreign power in opposition to US policy Nixon achieved his much-longed-for-victory. It was close – 43.42% to 42.72%. Had he not stopped Humphrey's momentum, by what LBJ called treasonous means, he would not have gained the slight edge that gave him his narrow victory.[49]

> "North Vietnam cannot defeat or humiliate the United States. Only Americans can do that."

Although an able politician Dick carried the baggage of his serious character flaws with him into the Oval Office. He frequently disregarded his mother's admonition to be honest and, in addition, frequently shared bigoted, homophobic and anti-Semitic sentiments with his staff.[50] [51]When he took office there were well over 500,000 Americans stationed in Vietnam and over 35,000 soldiers had been killed. Sure he had been a strong supporter of US involvement while he was Eisenhower's Vice President[52] but the responsibility for the war lay primarily with his Democratic predecessors.

Many people across the nation opposed the war. If he were to direct his representatives at the now resumed peace talks to simply work for a quick withdrawal that included a few face-saving concessions, such as returning our Prisoners of War (POWs), he, in all likelihood, would have been able to withstand the heat for the loss. He could have ended the war fairly quickly, perhaps within six months of taking office, and saved thousands and thousands of lives as did his mentor, President Eisenhower, who helped bring an end to the Korean War within six months of having entered office. It is probable that handled correctly and in time the American people would have understood. There were just two problems. One, Nixon did not want to be seen as a quitter. After all, his determination not to quit even after two major political defeats eventually brought him to the Oval Office.[53]

But the biggest obstacle was that Nixon actually believed that he could win. And after all, he was "not going to be the first American President to lose a war." Under JFK the hope was to build South Vietnam up into a position where they could keep their government together on their own in an effort to maintain a somewhat democratic stronghold in South East Asia. Under Johnson it was stopping the spread of communism at all costs and honoring the soldiers who had given their lives. Now it was personal; Nixon would not be seen as a quitter and he would not be humiliated by North Vietnam even if it meant the deaths of another 20,000 young Americans. Nixon decided to put a greater emphasis on the air war. Correspondingly, he widened the combat zone authorizing the secret bombing of neutral Cambodia. Cambodia had served as a safe haven for the enemy and possessed vital routes along the Ho Chi Minh trail.

In September of 1969 Ho died but this had little impact upon the prosecution of the war. Le Duan and his contemporaries were still waging their relentless, often murderous, campaign.

In order to gain support for his efforts Nixon appeared on television appealing to his base. He gave a speech wherein he called upon the "great silent majority" of Americans to support his efforts in Vietnam. Although the speech served to further divide a wounded nation his approval rating rose. This support gave Nixon the nerve to take more drastic action. With the assistance of the Central Intelligence Agency (CIA) a puppet leader ascended to power in Cambodia and Nixon gained authorization from him to invade with ground forces in April 1970.[54] When the American people learned of the invasion many were outraged over the war spreading into another country and protests broke out on college campuses all across the nation.[55] He soon ordered the troops to retreat to Vietnam.

When he realized that he could not win Nixon began the systematic withdrawal of ground troops, started to faze out the draft to quiet protesters and began to hand over the responsibility of the war to the South Vietnamese; a process he called Vietnamization.[56] He now proclaimed that the new objective of the war was to achieve "peace with honor."[57] According to Nixon the US would no longer do the fighting for those who would not defend themselves. This caused the troops that were left in the war zone to wonder why they were there if they were apparently not fighting to win. Morale began to rapidly sink. Obviously, who would want to die for a lost cause or for Richard Nixon to save face?

Nixon promised one of his top advisors, Henry Kissinger, that when given the chance he would really "punish" the North. As the peace talks ground on Dick weakened his negotiating position and said it would be all right if after US troops left the NVA remained in the parts of the South that they had conquered during the conflict. This basically guaranteed that communist forces would eventually completely overrun the South. Nixon just wanted a "decent interval" between the time the US left and the time that the North conquered the South. His main concern became securing the release of American POWs, a concession he could have achieved in 1969.

In October 1972 Kissinger announced that "peace is at hand."[58] Nixon hoped to end the war before the upcoming Presidential election but Thieu, fearing that he was being double-crossed, again backed out of the negotiations. Nevertheless, Nixon won his great victory capturing 49 States.[59] Then, as Christmas approached, he decided to mercilessly bomb the North to prove to Thieu that he could count on his support[60] into the future and to fulfill his sick need to "punish the enemy."[61]

Finally, Thieu was reassured and returned to the negotiating table. On January 24th, 1973 the US, South Vietnam, the NVA and the VC all agreed to stop fighting. The US would withdraw its combat troops from Vietnam and the North would release the American Prisoners of War.

The following year, as a result of his involvement in the Watergate cover-up, Nixon was forced to resign. A spirit of activism prevailed in America, without which it is doubtful that Congress would have pursued the criminal activities of Nixon with great vigor. When faced with the serious charges of high crimes, possible loss of his pension and other privileges as well as the chance of going to prison Nixon decided that quitting wasn't such a bad idea after all. 21,041 Americans were killed in Vietnam during his years in office.

Reflecting upon his former boss, Kissinger asked, "Can you imagine what this man would have been if someone had loved him? I don't think anybody ever did – not his parents, not his peers."[62]

Later, Nixon, looking for sympathy, had the nerve to present himself as the last victim of the Vietnam War as if he were being punished for the loss of the war and not because of his crimes and utter contempt for the Constitution.[63]

"... a war that is finished as far as America is concerned."

Gerald R. Ford was a Congressional Representative from Michigan when Nixon's Vice President Spiro Agnew was forced to resign for having taken bribes. Ford was the House Minority leader, honest, decent and well liked by colleagues.[64] The constitution called for the President to name a new VP and inasmuch as Ford had a good reputation and was trusted by both parties he was a natural choice for a divided nation still in shock from the revelation of all of the crimes in the White House. And so it was that Ford stepped up and became President when Nixon resigned and the final act of America's long involvement in the Vietnam War played out. Ford announced in an address to the students of Tulane University on April 23, 1975 that:

"Today, America can regain the sense of pride that existed before Vietnam. But it cannot be achieved by refighting a war that is finished as far as America is concerned. As I see it, the time has come to look forward to an agenda for the future, to unify, to bind up the Nation's wounds, and to restore its health and its optimistic self-confidence." [65]

The US would take no action when thousands of NVA and VC swarmed over the South and on April 30th ultimately charged right into the Presidential Palace in Saigon where they declared victory and the reunification of Vietnam under communist rule.[66] The war was now completely over and Saigon was renamed Ho Chi Minh City. The tolls were horrendous. 8 million tons of bombs had been dropped. An estimated three million civilian and military Vietnamese were killed.[67] Approximately 350,000 American soldiers were wounded[68] and more than 58,000 were dead.[69] America gave the war its best shot and, in the end, came up short.

Endnotes

1   William Doyle, *PT109 An American Epic of War, Survival and the Destiny of John F. Kennedy* (New York, N.Y.: Harper Collins Publishers, 2015) 98–110.

2   *IBID*, 159.

3   Chris Matthews, *Jack Kennedy Elusive Hero (New York, N.Y. Simon and Schuster, 2011)* 27-28.

4   White House Memorandum to the US Army, April 11, 1962.

5   Logevall, AI.

6   VANH, 210.

7   John Ketwig, *Vietnam Reconsidered: The War, the Times, and Why They Matter* (Trine Day LLC, 2019) 65-66. (Henceforth VR)

8   CBS TV Interview with President John F. Kennedy conducted by Walter Cronkite, September 2, 1963.

9   APH, 464.

10   VANH, 311.

11   *IBID*, 318.

12   TVW, 86.

13   Logevall, AI.

14   TVW, 94.

15   Logevall, AI.

16   McGeorge Bundy, AI, spring 1991.

17   VANH, 312.

18   Robert Dallek, *Lyndon B. Johnson: Portrait of a President* (Oxford University Press, 2004) 1. (Henceforth LBJ)

19   Cleve R. Wootson, Jr., "A History of White House Profanity – and one cursing presidential

parrot," *Washington Post*. www.wasingtonpost.com

20   VANH, 322.

21   LBJ, 176–179.

22   *IBID*, 179.

23   Logevall, AI.

24   LBJ, 188–189.

25   VANH, 321.

26   TVW, 108.

27   Logevall, AI.

28   VANH, 325.

29   TVW, 115–116.

30   VANH, 323-324.

31   Logevall, AI.

32   LBJ, 252, 258.

33   AWV, 90.

34   TVW, 246.

35   AWV, 115.

36   VANH, 332.

37   LBJ, 321–325.

38   David E. Sanger, "US General Considered Nuclear Response in Vietnam War, Cable Shows," *New York Times,* New York, N.Y. October 6, 2018.

39   Michael Beschloss, *Presidents of War* (New York, N.Y., Crown Publishing, 2018) 555.

40   LBJ, 332.

41   John A. Farrell, *Richard Nixon, The Life* (New York, N.Y., Doubleday Press, 2017) 532. (Henceforth RN)

42   *IBID*, 47.

43   *IBID*, 66-78.

44   Richard Nixon Presidential Library and Museum. Yorba Linda, CA.

45   H. R. Haldeman's Notes, *"-any other way to monkey wrench it?"* October 22, 1968. National Archives, Washington, D.C.

46   David F. Schmitz, *Richard Nixon and the Vietnam War* (Lanham, MD. Rowman and Little-field, 2016) 36–37. (Henceforth RNVW)

47   RN, 342–344.

48   RNVW, 36–37.

49   RN, 346.

50   *IBID*, 377–378.

51   *IBID*, 418, 426.

52   EOW, 491–493.

53   Richard Nixon resignation speech, August 8, 1974. *"I have never been a quitter. To leave office before my term is complete is abhorrent to every instinct in my body."*

54   Logevall, AI.

55   APH, 481.

56   *IBID*, 474.

57   VANH, 334.

58   RNVW, 40.

59   RN, 497.

60   VANH, 338.

61   David E. Hoffman, "Secret archive offers fresh insight into Nixon presidency," *Washington*

Post, October 11, 2015. www.washingtonpost.com

62 Jeff Shesol, "The Nixon Memorial," *The New Yorker.* August 6, 2014. www.newyorker.com

63 "Frost/Nixon Interview." Television broadcast. May 19, 1977.

64 RN, 519.

65 The History Place: Great Speeches Collection Gerald R. Ford "A War that is Finished" www.historyplace.com April 23, 1975.

66 VANH, 339.

67 Stanley Karnow, "Ho Chi Minh; He married nationalism to communism and perfected the deadly art of guerrilla warfare." April 1998. content.time.com

68 VR, 160.

69 Logevall, AI.

REARRANGING THEIR WORLD

*"Any woman who chooses to behave like a human being should be warned
that the armies of the status quo will treat her as something of a dirty joke.
That's their natural and first weapon. She will need her sisterhood."*
– Gloria Steinem, Activist, Journalist and a Feminist.

AWAKE AND RISE

In the early days of the Vietnam Era women were generally not encouraged to accomplish much of anything of real significance. Often they were directed to lower-level dead-end jobs and then were encouraged to quit when they married.[1] Men dominated the scene in politics, in business and in popular culture. There were no laws protecting women against discrimination in employment, education, health coverage, credit/banking and most other areas of life.[2]

Initially, some women gave the appearance of being content to be the force behind the man. Jacqueline Kennedy set the example of the "perfect" wife with her intelligence, glamour and style. This first lady served as a role model for millions of women across the United States. Women might work, mostly behind the scenes, to advance their husbands' careers and present themselves as a graceful partner as opposed to being seen as a subservient and stodgy housewife.[3]

JFK himself was not a champion of women's advancement, quite the contrary.[4] However, his powerful rhetoric concerning the responsibility of all Americans to serve their country and equality for all struck a chord in the hearts of many American women. JFK was their inspiration too whether he cared to be or not.

Starting in the 1950's America generally enjoyed unprecedented great wealth and so more women then ever were able to attend college and had developed high hopes for their future. However, many of these well-educated women married, moved to the suburbs and began to raise a family. As time went on her children grew and went off to school and Mom was left with little to do of any substance with the exception of domestic chores. Some of these women began to grow frustrated fast and wondered if their lives could not be made better by taking what was then considered some dramatic steps, such as finding a paying job.

Black women, particularly in the South, had taken a leading role in serving as a catalyst for the revolutionary changes that were about to take place in the United States. Rosa Parks, for instance, helped to start the Civil Rights movement by refusing to surrender her seat to a white man and move to the back of a bus in Montgomery, Alabama.[5] However, for the most part women were not allowed to take a front seat, so to speak, in the leadership of the Civil Rights movement; but their countless acts of courage in standing up to bigots resulted in bringing about the advances towards freedom and equality for all that were achieved during the Vietnam Era.[6]

Women began to speak up for themselves, enter the work force and change the way they were traditionally perceived, yet many Americans had trouble adjusting to this more progressive version of the female population. Some male employers did not want to give in and advance women, no matter how able they were, over men. In addition, it was thought that women often deserved less pay than did men because a man had to provide for his wife and children, never thinking that women also had families for which they provided. In addition, some job placement ads discriminated by sex with better paying jobs listed as for "men only."[7]

As the 60's advanced some women, especially among the young, who had been tied to fashion and high style, began to embrace the rebellious hippie movement. They often wore thrift store clothes and colorful psychedelic shirts. Make-up and good grooming went by the wayside in many cases. A young Hillary Rodham impressed her classmate Bill Clinton with her brilliant mind while wearing no make-up, a work shirt and jeans, had messy hair and coke-bottle eyeglasses.[8] Clinton had dated beauty queens in the past and his switch to Hillary spoke to the changing attitudes of the time.

College campuses became a hotbed of social unrest and women were a big part of the revolution. There were larger numbers then ever of young people attending colleges so these were places where they could get together and exchange ideas while far away from the influences of their hometown and their "old fashioned" parents. Yet many "progressive," leftist young men could not throw off their sexist attitudes. They frequently ignored women when they expressed their ideas and often insulted them and relegated them to the more mundane tasks associated with activism like routine clerical work and cleaning the office.[9]

Women began to realize that if they wanted to take a leadership role they would have to do it all by themselves. Everyday people, not only well known ones, led the movement. They were in the forefront on issues like equal opportunity in employment. Abortion was illegal in many States and many women organized their efforts to help others to find where they could obtain a safe abortion if they so desired.

Author and activist Betty Friedan started the National Organization of Women (NOW) to help provide legal aid for women who were discriminated against in the workplace. She quickly learned that there were many thousands of women in need of help. In addition, women began to organize demonstrations to change the way that they were looked upon and treated. A group of women protested the Miss America pageant in Atlantic City because they believed the event demeaned them as human beings. A reporter wrote that instead of burning their draft cards as some young men had done to protest the war, they burned their bras. This message became a symbol of what became known as the Women's Liberation Movement.[10]

Although activists made progress women realized that there was still a long way to go. But together they continued to make advancements.

UNWELCOME PATRIOTS

"When I was in the military, they gave me a medal for killing two men and a discharge for loving one."[11]
                    – Leonard Matlovich, A Gay Vietnam Veteran

From the days of the American Revolution through the Vietnam Era hundreds of thousands of gay women and men have served in the US Armed Forces. More often than not their sexual identity was kept a closely guarded secret. Often when someone was discovered to be gay she or he would be discharged, but not with honor. The first known case of someone being kicked out of the US military on account of homosexuality is that of Lieutenant Gotthold Frederick Enslin on March 11, 1778 at Valley Forge following a court martial presided over by the infamous Aaron Burr. Enslin was ceremoniously drummed out of the Army with the approval of no less than General George Washington himself.[12]

Over the many years gay military personnel were, naturally, not limited to male soldiers and sailors. Women are known to have served, for instance, in the Civil War disguised as men. Included among these courageous patriots were some who were lesbians.[13] Up until World War I women and men in the service were punished for engaging in homosexual acts, but later on people could be excluded from the military for simply having a homosexual orientation,[14] [15] and by 1943 the final regulations were in place to block gay people from entering all branches of the military.[16] Yet many continued to voluntarily enlist or respond to the draft without admitting to their true sexual nature.

Among the patriotic women volunteers in the service during the Vietnam Era there was a sizable contingent of lesbians. Periodically they were victims of what was known as a "witch-hunt." The Criminal Investigation Division (CID) would force one person believed to have participated in homosexual acts to give up the names of others and those would then be brought in to give up the names of more people to face interrogation and discharge.[17]

Neither were male volunteers exempt from punishment. In August of 1954 Navy Lieutenant (jg) Doctor Thomas A. Dooley began treating thousands of North Vietnamese civilians, many of whom were Catholic, fleeing to the south to escape communist persecution.[18] Dooley turned his experience into a best-selling book entitled *Deliver Us From Evil*. In it he praised the Navy for making possible the medical assistance offered to the refugees. When it was reported to the Office of Naval Intelligence (ONI) that the now famous Doctor was secretly an active gay man they responded swiftly, offering him an immediate separation without fanfare.[19] He would say that he was returning to Southeast Asia as a civilian to continue his work among the indigenous population and the terms of his Undesirable Discharge would remain a secret.[20] [21] The Navy would not suffer from "bad" publicity and Dr. Dooley would not be subjected to further disrespect and humiliation.[22] [23] [24]

Dooley did continue his good works and to write about them until his death from cancer in January 1961 at the age of 34. His example served to help inspire JFK to create the Peace Corps.[25]

During the Vietnam Era many young men feigned homosexuality in order to dodge military service. On the other hand, as the military became desperate for soldiers it would occasionally look the other way, particularly if the prospective recruit had no objection to serving.[26] For instance, Perry Watkins was taught never to lie and when asked at the induction center if he were gay he quite naturally responded, "Yes." And when asked if he would serve in Vietnam if necessary he again responded, "Yes." The Army psychiatrist marked him fit for duty and Perry was off to Basic Combat Training. Watkins noted that white draftees who reported that they were gay were rejected but he thought that because he was a black man he was compelled to serve.

He was not sent to Vietnam but instead was stationed in Germany where he worked in personnel and was not ashamed to be openly gay. He had his share of troubles as he literally fought off homophobes but even in this atmosphere he managed to excel. Sometimes, while off duty, he even walked around the base in drag. He entertained the troops in USO shows dressed as famous women and enthusiastically lip-synced their popular songs to rousing applause, laughter and cheers. Perry was such an exemplary soldier that he was not criticized but instead regularly promoted. He was friendly, intelligent, wise and personable and so he was well liked and earned the respect of many of his comrades.[27]

Watkins loved his military experience and re-enlisted several times before, with the war over and the army no longer desperate for troops, he was discharged because of his sexual orientation.[28] [29]Both Dr. Dooley and Sergeant First Class Perry Watkins were fantastic service members yet were senselessly punished for who they naturally were as human beings. Gay military personnel that wanted to survive their experience and receive an honorable discharge were forced to live secret lives. Some were beaten up or sexually assaulted by their "buddies" when their orientation was discovered or even simply suspected.

THE CRUEL IRONY

"I will not disgrace my religion, my people or myself by becoming a tool to enslave those who are fighting for their own justice, freedom and equality... "[30]

– Muhammad Ali, World Champion Boxer

Throughout American history, black women and men have frequently been oppressed and targeted by haters and bigots. Whenever there was a war many African-Americans looked upon it as an opportunity to prove their devotion to their country. From America's earliest days to the time of Frederick Douglass and the Civil War and well into the Twentieth Century they hoped that serving in the military would help them to gain their rightful equal place in society. Vietnam was no different, at first.[31] In the early days of the war many Civil Rights leaders were hesitant to break with Lyndon Johnson's efforts in Vietnam because of all of the assistance he had provided to the movement and hopefully would continue to provide. However, there was a growing faction of African-American activists that started questioning the non-violent and cooperative approach to equal rights and began to become more militant and unafraid of alienating important establishment figures. Malcolm X, for instance, was an early critic of black participation in the war.[32]

Important African-American organizations like The Congress of Racial Equality (CORE) and The Student Non Violent Coordinating Committee (SNCC) began to more actively support the antiwar movement. In April 1965 SNCC's executive committee supported a large rally in Washington, D.C. organized by the leftist Students for a Democratic Society (SDS).

From the Gulf of Tonkin to the return of the POWs in 1973 the United States spent an estimated 111 billion dollars to conduct the war and many billions more to help the South Vietnamese and other allies. Great Society programs that were designed to help, among others, Americans who were down trodden due in part to institutional racism received far less funding. For example, a total of 5 billion dollars was allocated from 1964 to 1966 for LBJ's "war on poverty."[33]

Once in the service African-Americans faced a discriminatory environment. The military justice system, for instance, was far harsher on black offenders than on whites. Close to 40 percent of African-Americans convicted of having gone Absent Without Leave (AWOL) were sentenced to jail time as opposed to 15 percent of white offenders. One study showed that 50 percent of all prisoners held in pretrial confinement in West Germany were black but made up less than 10 percent of the enlisted strength in that country. In addition, African-American soldiers were more likely to be court martialed for lesser offenses than were whites.[34] All new recruits were tested to determine their qualification for a particular Military Occupational Status (MOS). The tests were supposed to be culturally neutral but in reality contained a Eurocentric bias.[35] The National Association for the Advancement of Colored People (NAACP) deemed it, "a bonus for growing up white." Poorer testing African-American service members were relegated in large numbers to service and supply units and to the infantry.[36] In 1965 25% of all enlisted men's combat deaths were those of black soldiers. The Defense Department was so embarrassed by this statistic that they developed a posting system to significantly lower the percentage.[37]

As the conflict progressed and attitudes towards the war began to become more divided, young black draftees grew increasingly sensitive to the racism in their military experience. They would find few champions among the upper ranks inasmuch as only 2% of all officer's were black. In response African-American enlisted men tended to stick together and develop a black culture within the military. Some soldiers would greet one another with a clenched fist raised to shoulder level or by an elaborate handshake called a "dap" and associate only with other black soldiers while off duty.[38]

In early 1967 Dr. Martin Luther King, Jr., no longer able to restrain himself, spoke out forcefully against the war. He said, "…when the guns of war become a national obsession, social needs inevitably suffer."[39] He began to encourage young black men to avoid the service. "We have been repeatedly faced with the cruel irony of watching Negro and white boys on TV screens as they kill and die together for a nation that has been unable to seat them together in the same schools."[40] Dr. King's murder in April of 1968 contributed to the greater alienation of black service members from the military system. Meanwhile, in Oakland, California residents Bobby Seale (later one of the Chicago 8) and Huey Newton founded The Black Panther Party for Self Defense. Sick of instances where the police came into their neighborhood and harassed black people, the two young African-Americans decided to put the police on notice. California law permitted citizens to openly carry firearms. Whenever a police officer pulled over a black woman or man the Panthers would soon arrive on the scene to make sure that the police did not mistreat the person that they had stopped. Panthers would stand a short distance away and appear intimidating in their black berets, leather jackets and black sunglasses with shotguns or other rifles at the ready. Panthers opposed the war in Vietnam because they believed that it was just an effort by the US to colonize a foreign land. They sympathized with the Viet Cong and identified with them. The Panthers saw themselves as a colonized people living in the white man's America. They called for revolution, violent if necessary because they had had enough of Dr. King's vision of nonviolence and joining hands and singing hymns. They popularized the phrases "Black is beautiful," "Power to the people" and christened the police "Pigs." The Panthers became prevalent on a national scale with chapters in every major and many smaller cities in America. Although they successfully created social service programs (i.e. free breakfast for children) the Black Panthers became involved in a number of shootouts with the police resulting in many casualties on both sides. Radical Black Panther leaders would recruit African-American veterans and even active duty soldiers.[41]

"… PAY ANY PRICE, BEAR ANY BURDEN…"

"He's not a war hero. He's a war hero because he was captured. I like people that weren't captured."[42]
 – Donald Trump disparaging John McCain's Vietnam service.

Three future Presidents were the perfect age to have served in Vietnam. None went. In fact they did everything that they could to prevent their going. Bill Clinton mostly took advantage of student deferments. George W. Bush entered the National Guard where he served part-time and was guaranteed not to have to leave the USA. Donald Trump used student status for a while and later managed to parley a fake foot condition into a medical deferment.

On the other hand someone who would become an important political figure and *had* gone to Vietnam was John McCain. McCain came from a highly successful military family. He attended The United States Naval Academy at Annapolis where he enjoyed the dubious distinction of finishing nearly last in his class. McCain was way too busy joking around to take his schoolwork seriously, but his sobering wake-up call came when an aircraft carrier upon which he was serving, USS *Forrestal*, caught on fire and 134 of his shipmates perished. Another 161 were injured.

Late in 1967 he was flying a bombing mission over Hanoi when his plane was struck by anti-aircraft fire, tearing away the right wing, but McCain managed to eject, breaking both of his arms and a leg in the effort. He dropped into a lake and was captured immediately by local Vietnamese. Once on shore the seriously injured pilot was kicked, stabbed with a bayonet and beaten by civilians until, ironically, NVA soldiers came to his rescue. In the coming years there would be times when he may have wished that he hadn't survived that crash. McCain was held at first in what the other POWs sarcastically referred to as the Hanoi Hilton, an old French prison in the heart of the North Vietnamese capital. He was frequently tortured and for at least two years was held in solitary confinement.

When the Vietnamese realized that McCain's father was an important high-ranking Naval official they offered to release him to gain propaganda points. However, the military code of conduct stated that prisoners would be released in chronological order. Those who were there the longest would be released first. There were other soldiers and sailors who had been incarcerated longer than McCain and so as a point of honor he refused to be set free. He would suffer many more months of torture and deprivation. The fun-loving boy who finished nearly last in his class had transformed into a heroic man.[43]

When the US participation in the war finally ended in 1973 McCain had served five and a half years in prison and so at long last he and his fellow POWs were returned to the USA. The effects of his wounds were so severe that he was eventually unable to continue his military career and soon ran for political office. He wound up as a Senator from Arizona.[44] This, however, was not enough for the patriotic and ambitious veteran. He wanted to go all the way. He wanted to be President.

Another future politician with real courage and patriotism was John Kerry. Kerry was raised in a privileged household. He attended the best schools and traveled widely. Upon graduation from Yale he too joined the Navy. Inspired by John F. Kennedy's challenge to "pay any price, bear any burden" Kerry volunteered for the war zone, writing "...I consider the opportunity to serve in Vietnam as an extremely important part of being in the armed forces..." He further requested that he be assigned to a Shallow Water Inshore Fast Tactical (SWIFT) boat. Both of his requests were honored.[45]

While in Vietnam he conducted himself in a heroic fashion. He was wounded three times and nearly killed on numerous occasions, he saved a shipmates life, engaged in mortal combat with the enemy and for his actions earned three Purple Hearts, a Bronze Star with a "V" for valor and a Silver Star. After being wounded a third time, following regulations, he was ordered to return home. Upon reflection Kerry began to believe that the war was wrong. He was angry over what he;

> "...had seen the war do to the young men who served, over the neglect and even rejection of returning warriors, over the deception, the outright lies that had been told for years by government officials and top military brass about the war itself, and the tactics and strategy – if they could be called that – which resulted in unnecessary dying and killing in Vietnam for more years than anyone anticipated – and for what?"[46]

After he was discharged he became active with a group called Vietnam Veterans Against the War (VVAW). He attended a conference in which many of his fellow veterans enumerated atrocities that they said they had witnessed or in which they had participated.[47] During a demonstration in Washington, D.C. Kerry was asked to address the members of the Senate Foreign Relations Committee in the Capitol Building on the topic of VVAW's outlook. Kerry, in a fatigue shirt, testified. As spokesman for the group he recited a litany of cruelty that the other vets had reported and then he said, "How do you ask a man to be the last man to die in Vietnam? How do you ask a man to be the last man to die for a mistake?"[48]

He concluded his eloquent statement by saying "...when, in thirty years from now, our brothers go down the street without a leg, without an arm or a face, and small boys ask why, we will be able to say 'Vietnam' and not mean a desert, not a filthy obscene memory, but mean instead the place where America finally turned and where soldiers like us helped it in the turning."[49]

Kerry went on to become a successful politician and he too began to dream of one day becoming President. He served in the Upper House with

John McCain. The two men certainly held no animosity towards each other but they did look upon one another, at first, with "suspicion and mistrust."[50] What is more McCain was a Republican and Kerry a Democrat. Yet the two were able to find common ground in their Vietnam experience and became loyal friends. They worked together on a committee to resolve the issue of whether or not POWs were still being held in Vietnam. During this investigation, which determined that there were no American prisoners left in Vietnam, McCain suffered insults at the hands of people who were selling tee-shirts and flags that earned profits from the perpetuation of the POW myth through playing on the pitiable hopes of the families of a missing and in fact deceased service member. He was smeared as a "Manchurian candidate." That is to say a person who was held by the enemy and brainwashed to return to America and work against it. The smear campaign was effective and was resurrected to hurt McCain's efforts to gain the Republican nomination for President against George W. Bush in 2000. Although Kerry and fellow Vietnam veterans in the Senate came to his defense the lie contributed to his losing the nomination.[51] [52]

When Kerry made his run for the White House in 2004 similar tactics were used to spoil his chances. Opponents maliciously claimed that Kerry was a fraud. McCain supported Kerry's Vietnam record but no matter how much support he had or proof was presented to show that he was a true hero the smears continued.[53] [54] Kerry's effort also ended in failure.

Apparently many Americans were willing to look upon Vietnam veterans such as McCain and Kerry as mentally disturbed and/or phonies. The stigmas played on the vestiges of the need to blame someone for the war's loss and their political opponents capitalized on that need.

Out Now!

"All you need is love."
– John Lennon, Beatle and a Peacenik

Jane Fonda was a very popular movie star who also happened to be an antiwar activist. She was married to Tom Hayden, an important member of SDS and one of the group known as the Chicago 8.

During the war Fonda traveled to locations near military bases where she and her troupe presented "Free The Army" (FTA) shows that were made up largely of song, dance and comedy to entertain the soldiers. Her satirical performances were designed to encourage the GI's to seriously question their involvement in the war.[55]

If this were basically the extent of her involvement her role as an activist may have been largely dismissed when the war at last came to a conclusion. However, she did one more thing of note; in July of 1972 she traveled to North Vietnam. Jane saw her trip as a fact-finding mission and a chance for an American to extend a wish for peace to the North Vietnamese. The Vietnamese, meanwhile, were more than happy to use her visit for propaganda purposes. Her biggest mistake came when she was filmed sitting astride an enemy anti-aircraft gun, which was the same type of weapon that was used to shoot American planes along with its crew out of the sky.

When she returned home she was harshly critical of American POWs, speaking of them in a highly disrespectful and insensitive manner. Years later, although not sorry for her opposition to the war, she would repeatedly and profusely apologize for her cruel, ignorant and inconsiderate behavior – but for a group of people it wasn't enough and never could be. Some people even called for "Hanoi Jane," as she was derisively nicknamed, to be tried as a traitor to the United States; to lock her up and then to literally execute her.

Most of those who spoke out against the war have long since been forgiven or even praised. Antiwar veteran John Kerry, for instance, was elected to the Senate, served as Secretary of State and was even his party's nominee for President. Bill Clinton, an anti Vietnam War draft resister, was even elected to the Presidency. Twice! Donald Trump, who pretended that he had a sore foot to dodge military service, also managed to make it to the Oval Office.

Over 300 American civilians, some quite well known, had ventured to North Vietnam before Jane yet there has been no hue and cry for their arrest, incarceration and execution. Their act is, for the most part, forgotten and therefore as good as forgiven. But not Jane's. Fonda's visit to Vietnam had zero effect on the outcome of the war because it was about six months away from the official handing over of the fighting to the South Vietnamese. Not many service members heard her because her radio broadcasts were jammed and there were relatively few American soldiers in Vietnam at that time. The limited number of POWs that were able to hear her broadcasts were, for the most part, unaffected. Some already agreed that the war was wrong and others were so tough that no one could demoralize them, especially a lone movie actor.

Urban legend has it that she caused the death of three POWs because she reported them to the NVA for trying to pass their Social Security number to her. The seven POWs that she met with sat before TV and movie cameras and, therefore, had no need to surreptitiously pass identification inasmuch as one need only to look at the films to know with whom she spoke. The enemy never punished the POWs for anything that happened during Fonda's visit.[56]

After the war was over and lost a number of people felt the need to find a scapegoat. Some said it was the politician's fault for "tying the hands of the soldiers in the battlefield." Others blamed the protesters for lending aid and comfort to the enemy. But neither one of those arguments could succinctly summarize the degree of bitterness that was harbored over the defeat. There are those who believe, perhaps unconsciously, that their masculinity was in question because they were unable to win. As a defense they blamed femininity, something they equated with weakness, for the loss.[57]

Jane Fonda was nothing if not feminine. None of the other women visitors to North Vietnam were as beautiful and as famous as was Fonda, thereby making her an easy choice for her unfortunate eternal scapegoat status.[58] Many years after the war Fonda was signing books when a cowardly man spat in the unsuspecting 67-year-old woman's face before he quickly scurried away. When security caught up with the pitiable assailant he claimed that his act was revenge for her activities during the war.[59] [60]

Daniel Berrigan was with just a small handful of people when he first protested against the war in Vietnam in Washington, D.C. Eventually he would see that handful grow to hundreds of thousands, due in part to his influence. Along with his brother, Philip, he was a radical antiwar activist who opposed US involvement in Vietnam and who also happened to be a Roman Catholic Priest of the Jesuit Order.[61] His actions, sermons and writings would inspire many but most especially young Catholics. Father Berrigan was an outstanding intellectual and an excellent poet as well as earnest and kind. These attributes are what drew others to him. Not to mention that he had the "guts" to really challenge authority. He and Philip were the first Catholic priests to be arrested and sentenced to prison for opposing the war.

Prior to his incarceration Daniel and historian Howard Zinn flew to Hanoi on a "mission of peace" in 1968. The North Vietnamese, as a gesture of good will, as a propaganda tool and in an effort to strengthen support of antiwar groups released three POWs into their custody. These were the first prisoners held in the North to be set free during the war.[62] [63] [64]Not long after Daniel's Vietnam trip the Berrigan brothers and seven other Catholics burned draft files in Catonsville, Maryland, using homemade napalm. Daniel said, "Apologies, good friends, for the fracture of good order, the burning of paper instead of children ..."[65]

The Catonsville Nine, as they became known, were convicted of destruction of government property, interference with the Selective Service Act and destruction of Selective Service files. After eluding the authorities for four months he was placed on the FBI's "Most Wanted" list and was at last captured. Father Berrigan was sent away and served two years in a Federal Penitentiary.[66]

Paul **Booth** was a teenager attending Swarthmore College in Pennsylvania and majoring in political science when he founded a chapter of SDS. A number of his associates in the group were quite militant but Paul differed because he believed that although demonstrations were important the answer to many of the problems that America faced could best be solved by supporting  mainstream candidates or by running for political office themselves.

Paul was a "cheerful spirit" in the organization, he would often sing or tell stories to maintain morale during tempestuous, complicated meetings and organizational sessions. Before long Paul became the national spokesman for Students for a Democratic Society and as such organized the first significant demonstration in Washington, D.C., attracting more than 25,000 people in 1965 when US combat troops had only been in Vietnam for a few months. The parade stretched from the Washington monument to the Capitol building and was followed by picketing at the White House.[67]

Instead of "Burn, Baby, Burn" Paul tried to popularize the saying "Build, Not Burn" meaning people should be given the opportunity to perform a public service instead of military service. He wanted to allow people to build something worthwhile for our country instead of being compelled to burn their draft card as some war resisters did. Paul believed that the war in Vietnam was destroying the chance to solve domestic problems such as poverty and racial discrimination.[68]

Paul, along with Lee Webb, another SDS member, wrote;

> "To our assertion of the dignity of individuals, of the values of love, honesty, reason, and equality, America responds with war, manipulation, and the selfish concentration of wealth. The America which we face denies democracy – it is a nation in which the crucial economic decisions which affect us all are made by corporate managers and bankers, in which millions of people are dependent on the indulgence of public welfare systems over which they have no control, in which the decisions of war and peace are made by a clique of advisers and experts. Can this be called democracy? We understand democracy to be that system of rule in which the people make the decisions that effect their lives… the times demand that the movement against the war become a movement for domestic social change."[69]

The Whole World Is Watching

"All you kiddies remember to lay off the needle drugs, the only dope worth shooting is Richard Nixon."[70]

Abbie Hoffman (below), Radical Activist
and a Founder of the Yippies

They were troublemakers, outrageous and fresh. They were pranksters, funny and silly. They were irreverent and disrespectful wisenheimers. They were instigators, revolutionaries and radicals. They were YIPPIES!

When founded they imagined changing everything by harnessing the energy of young people from around the globe, particularly hippies, and spawn a "revolution for the hell of it." After all, they were sick and tired of the capitalist economic system that they believed brought about the war in Vietnam, racist subjugation and poverty and it was time to end it once and forever.

Like the Diggers of San Francisco before them the Yippies were a radical political street theater group. Their first act of note was a prank at the New York Stock Exchange. Wall Street, they believed, was the very engine of the war machine. A "stoned" Stew Albert (left with Judy Gumbo), Jerry Rubin (right), Abbie Hoffman and a handful of other Yippies went up into the visitors' gallery

and proceeded to throw dollar bills down on the stockbrokers, clerks and runners – thereby creating a mad scramble. Many shouted, pointed fingers and shook their fists at the small group of intruders while others ran over to gather up the loot. When the money stopped fluttering down the crowd below booed and the Yippies were hustled away by security.

Downstairs, the media, having been told in advance that there was an action planned, interviewed Hoffman and Rubin, in particular, who used the attention to put forth their statements. To the delight of the photographers present the two ceremoniously burned a five-dollar bill. The next day reports of their demonstration appeared in newspapers including the venerable *New York Times*, which served to encourage the Yippie leaders. Quick to learn, they developed into successful media manipulators.[71][72]

Yippies were an outgrowth of the Hippie movement. Hippies were comprised of millions of Baby Boomers who valued sex, drugs and rock and roll. Most smoked marijuana and believed in the wonders of LSD as encouraged by Harvard Psychologist Dr. Timothy Leary. These peaceful "flower children" were largely apolitical living a lifestyle that rejected greed and militarism, thereby posing a threat to the dominant culture. The Yippies attempted to politicize this phenomenal movement.

Highly motivated and optimistic about their ability to influence the war effort the Yippies participated in organizing a huge demonstration in Washington, D.C. culminating in a march on the Pentagon where they claimed that by magic and witchcraft and all manner of mumbo-jumbo the building would be levitated and exorcised. They also said that they would turn the Potomac River red, put LSD in the city's water supply and burn the famous cherry trees. None of those claims materialized but all of them were crazy enough to end up in newspaper and television reports. The Yippies received the attention that they craved. Perhaps a hundred thousand people showed up for the demonstration in D.C. and an estimated 35 to 50 thousand of those people marched on the Pentagon where armed soldiers confronted them and literally beat them back. A plan to "bomb" D.C. by plane with hundreds of daises was foiled and so the demonstrators distributed the flowers by hand. A few were placed in the barrels of the soldiers' guns.

Although it is unclear what effect they had on the government's position on the war it appeared to have changed the tactics and attitude of some of the antiwar movement from passive protest to more active resistance.[73]

A third and probably the most significant act of note began in the streets of Chicago. For the most part it started out as a harmless and peaceful protest including the Yippie's satirical act of nominating an actual pig for President. Some Yippies and their supporters tried to and sometimes did engage the National Guardsmen in intelligent discussion; however, some people threw rocks at police and waved Vietcong flags. Demonstrators ended up in a major battle with the boiling mad Chicago's "finest" who positively hated the antiwar activists. With TV cameras rolling and protesters chanting, "The whole world is watching," police marched into the thick of a crowd of demonstrators and began to brutally beat them with fists and clubs before dragging many away to face arrest.

Neither side realized, perhaps, how much they had in common. Some of the police were themselves avoiding the draft; their occupation considered necessary they were exempted from military service; some were veterans and some had close relatives that were either killed, wounded or were serving in Vietnam. On the other side among the protesters some too avoided the draft, college students for instance were exempted, some were veterans and some had close relatives that were either killed, wounded or were serving in Vietnam.[74] After the smoke cleared Abbie Hoffman and Jerry Rubin along with six others, initially dubbed the Chicago 8, were charged with conspiracy to form a riot. The trial was much celebrated in the press while the two Yippies made a mockery of the court's proceedings, showing up for trial one day in judicial robes and on another wearing a Chicago policeman's uniform, for example.

Some of the women including Abbie Hoffman's wife Anita, Jerry Rubin's girlfriend Nancy Kurshan and Tasha, the daughter of another defendant, Dave Dellinger, formed a group that they called the Women's International Terrorist Conspiracy from Hell, or WITCH. At the end of the trial the group dressed up like witches and put a curse on the Judge while burning judge's robes. It was all part of the attention-grabbing street theater of the Yippies.[75] Despite the "curse" the Yippies were convicted and sentenced to five years in prison, but the verdict was overturned when it was determined that it was not a riot caused by them but rather by the police![76]

Hoffman and Rubin always contended that if the authorities had just ignored them no one would ever have heard of them. Ironically, in their effort to silence the radicals the "establishment" made them famous.[77]

VIOLENT REVOLUTION

"You don't need a weatherman to know which way the wind blows."
– Bob Dylan

When SDS first started out it modeled itself after African American activist groups like the Congress of Racial Equality (CORE) and the Student Non Violent Coordinating Committee (SNCC). As time went on some of the SDS leadership began to abandon the non-violent strategy in performing civil disobedience and began to call for more confrontational action.

Following the takeover of five buildings on the Columbia University campus in New York in April of '68 the more radical faction of SDS grew emboldened.[78] When SDS met in Detroit in June of '69 the militant faction basically hijacked the convention. With much of the leadership of the society, among them Bernadine Dohrn (above left), Bill Ayers (above right), Mark Rudd and Terry Robbins embracing violence and breaking from the rest of the group SDS began to fall apart.[79]

The great majority of the tens of thousands of members did not wish to be a part of the faction that emerged. That faction christened themselves the "Weatherman." One of the group's first acts was to call for "Days of Rage." They wanted thousands and thousands of young people to mass in Chicago at the beginning of the Chicago 8 trial and riot in the streets causing destruction and engaging the police in pitched battles. However, when the night came for the first such effort the numbers that they had hoped for did not materialize and they were lucky to have a few hundred young people wearing football helmets and armed with bats and rocks willing to "take to the streets." [80]

At this point they might have gotten the message that their tactic was not a popular one and would not work. Instead, they thought they had to ratchet up the violence in their vain hopes of sparking a national armed revolution. Using a townhouse in New York's Greenwich Village as the assembly point, members of the Weatherman faction began to put together bombs meant to be used to blow up a Fort Dix, New Jersey Non Commissioned Officer's (NCO) dance with the intention of killing as many soldiers and their guests as possible in an effort to "bring the war home."[81] However, a bomb accidently exploded in the townhouse and instantly killed three members of the organization, including Terry Robbins, and completely destroyed the building.

The death of their three comrades badly shook the membership. Already in deep trouble for instigating the riot in Chicago, among other things some members thought it prudent to go "underground." Meaning they would live life under assumed identities and avoid capture by the authorities while conducting antiwar activities. Others took it as their cue to drop out of the organization all together and return to more traditional methods of protest. Now a small cadre, they became known as the Weather Underground Organization (WUO). The leadership had lost its taste for murder but still wanted to take the battle to the establishment. They started to plant bombs but would first alert the occupants of the building they targeted so that they could get out before the thing detonated.

Over the next few years they bombed the Pentagon, NYPD headquarters and the Capitol Building among others, for a total of about 25 attacks in which no one is believed to have been killed or wounded. In addition, the WUO aided in the escape of LSD guru Dr. Timothy Leary from the penitentiary. But after a while it became apparent that their actions were having little or no effect on influencing the American people to join them in a violent uprising to overthrow the government of the United States and its Capitalist system.

The FBI foolishly violated the Constitutional rights of many radical organizations in the United States, including the WUO, by instituting a program called COINTELPRO and illegally wiretapping phones; searching homes of family members of the fugitives without a warrant among other illegal tactics. The result was that they destroyed all opportunities to charge the bombers with any serious offenses. Following the end of the war many of the fugitives began to resurface. By the late 70's and early 80's most had surrendered. They faced only fines, probation or short jail sentences.

Two members, Kathy Boudin and David Gilbert, refused to give up the cause and joined with a faction of the Black Panther Party called the Black Liberation Army (BLA). During the robbery of a Brink's truck by the group two policemen and a guard were murdered. Boudin served 22 years for her part in the crime and Gilbert is in prison to this day and is expected to be there for the rest of his life.[82]

AMERICA, LOVE IT OR LEAVE IT

"As for those deserters, malcontents, radicals, incendiaries, the civil and uncivil disobedients among the young, SDS, PLP, Weathermen I and Weathermen II, the revolutionary action movement, the Black United Front, Yippies, Hippies, Yahoos, Black Panthers, Lions and Tigers alike - I would swap the whole damn zoo for a single platoon of the kind of young Americans I saw in Vietnam."
– Spiro T. Agnew, Vice President of the United States[83]

Members of the Johnson Administration made a conscious decision not to enlist the backing of Hollywood moviemakers or conduct big rallies, fundraisers and parades supporting the troops as was done in World War II because they didn't want to draw too much attention to the war. They feared that it might raise debate followed by opposition. As the war escalated opposition did grow and the "counter-culture" began to draw a lot of attention. Most Americans, especially early on, supported the President's efforts in Vietnam and many developed a literal hatred for the mostly young people who grew their hair long and expressed opinions that members of the "silent majority" felt were in direct opposition to traditional American values. Many looked upon these "baby boomers" as an over-privileged and ungrateful generation. There were those who would have liked nothing better than to punch one or two "hippie freaks" right square in the nose.

But many Americans only wanted to present an opposing argument to the antiwar demonstrations. They yearned to wave "Old Glory" and sing time-honored songs of patriotism while supporting the troops, as was done in the "good old days." What they hated most was when someone burned an American flag; although few people ever actually burnt the flag it made for big sales when a newspaper ran a shock-inducing photo of an American flag in flames on the front page as opposed to some hippie holding up the two-fingered peace sign or offering a soldier a flower, for instance. Also, some demonstrators carried the flag of the Vietcong, which quite understandably infuriated plenty of people.

At last, on a sunny day in May of 1967, about 75,000 people marched down Fifth Avenue in Manhattan to demonstrate their support for the war. They believed that the "boys" in Vietnam would experience a "one hundred percent" morale boost when they learned that the parade had taken place. The huge crowd of men, women and children was comprised of marching bands and veterans as well as labor union representatives and regular folks from schools, churches and hospitals. Many carried the star-spangled banner while others held signs that read things like "My Country Right or Wrong," "Escalate Don't Capitulate" and "Hey, Hey What Do You Say? Let's Support the USA."

To add to the festivities two men carrying American flags parachuted into Central Park to a spot where a flag had recently been burned. A policeman apologized to them for having to issue a summons. Back on Fifth Avenue the crowd on the sidewalk burst into applause and cheers when they saw hundreds of off-duty policemen marching in plainclothes with their shields pinned to their jackets while others proudly wore their uniform.

Yet, when the police that were assigned to the parade route tried to stop assaults by a few of the participants upon people who disagreed with their point of view the police were roughed up. In another instance a group of people threw eggs and beer cans at an apartment building from which a sheet was flying with an inscription: "US get out of Vietnam." Meanwhile, one long-haired young man wearing sandals was smeared with motor oil and feathers and beaten by a gang of about thirty men shouting, "Get him, kill him, he's a beatnik, he burned our flag." Police Officer Daniel Ryan ran over to help "this kid." He reported, "They started belting him and me with tar. And then they threw feathers on us."

But these acts were committed by only a small number of participants. By far the vast majority wanted to show their support in a traditionally patriotic way of singing songs that praised America and marching peacefully.[84] [85] [86]

It was a very different scene a few years later when, frustrated with the persistence of the antiwar movement, an estimated two hundred construction workers wearing their hardhats rushed into a crowd of antiwar protesters on Manhattan's Wall Street and proceeded to beat them up. They blackened eyes, bloodied noses and broke bones while they rampaged in small groups; some armed with pipes and tools and shouting things like, "Kill the commie bastards!" and "America, Love it or Leave it!" Witnesses reported that in some cases the police stood by, perhaps afraid of the hardhats or in sympathy with them, and made no attempt to put a stop to the assaults. The mob made its way to City Hall where they demanded that the flag be raised from half-staff, having been lowered in memory of four students who were killed by the National Guard at an antiwar rally on Ohio's Kent State campus. Workers vaulted barricades and stormed past the policemen who stood guard at the front doors. Overwhelmed, frightened and uncertain of what else to do the police asked the Deputy Mayor to order that the flag be raised.

As the flag went up, the workers began singing the National Anthem. A "hardhat" shouted an order to the police to, "Get your helmets off." Grinning sheepishly, about 7 of the 15 police who were on the City Hall steps, removed their helmets. These young construction workers were self-proclaimed patriots that clearly loved the flag and intensely supported the war. They were strong and healthy and professed to hate draft dodgers – which begs the question, why wasn't even a single one of them in Vietnam? [87] [88] [89]

A few weeks later another rally supporting the war was held in the Wall Street area drawing tens of thousands of non-violent supporters. Hundreds of on-duty uniformed policemen marched at the rear of the parade. This led some spectators to believe that the police had joined the demonstration. A Department spokesman offered that they were there only as a "reserve" in case of disorders when the parade broke up. [90] [91]

Endnotes

1   Gail Collins, *When Everything Changed*. (New York, N.Y.; Little, Brown and Company, 2010) 15-17. (Henceforth WEC)

2   Heather Booth, AI, March 2019.

3   WEC, 40-42.

4   *IBID*, 66-67.

5   *IBID*, 108–109.

6   *IBID*, 119.

7   Booth, AI.

8   Bill Clinton, *My Life*. (New York, N.Y.; Vintage Books, 2005) 182–183.

9   Todd Gitlin, *The Sixties Years of Hope, Days of Rage*. (New York, N.Y.; Bantam Book, 1993) 363. (Henceforth SYH)

10   WEC 192–194.

11   Tombstone epitaph of Leonard Matlovich, Congressional Cemetery, Washington, D.C., June 1988.

12   Randy Shilts, *Conduct Unbecoming: Gays and Lesbians in the US Military, Vietnam to the Persian Gulf* (New York, N.Y.: Saint Martin's Press, 1993) 11–12. (Henceforth CU)

13   *IBID*, 14.

14   Chuck Stewart, *Gay and Lesbian Issues: A Reference Handbook* (Santa Barbara, CA.: ABC-CLIO; Annotated edition, 2003) 4-5.

15   CU, 15.

16   *IBID*, 16.

17   *IBID*, 181-182.

18   Boyle, Al.

19   James T. Fisher, *Dr. America: The Lives of Thomas A. Dooley 1927–1961* (Amherst, MA: University of Massachusetts Press, 1997) 26-27, 83–84, 87–89.

20   Diana Shaw, "The Temptation of Tom Dooley," *Los Angeles Times,* December 15, 1991. 50, 80.

21   Gay and Lesbian Alumni (GALA) of Notre Dame and St. Mary's. *The Thomas A. Dooley Award. "... for (sic) his humanitarian work as an American 'jungle doctor' in Laos subsequent to his undesirable discharge from the Navy."*

22   Wayne McKinny, MD, "Doctor would have been glad," *Desert Sun,* Palm Springs, California, January 8, 2011. 29.

23   John DeGregorio, "An American Hero Who Was Gay; Tom Dooley Would Have Been A Powerful Role Model If Society Had Let Him," *St. Louis Post-Dispatch,* St. Louis, Missouri, April 25, 1993. 13.

24   CU 23–24.

25   Tim O'Neil, "A Look Back - The jungle doctor, Tom Dooley, succumbs to cancer in 1961," *St. Louis Post-Dispatch,* January 18, 2014.

26   Nathaniel Frank, *Unfriendly Fire: How the Gay Ban Undermines The Military and Weakens America* (New York, N.Y. Saint Martin's Press, 2009) 229.

27   Perry Watkins, Al, January 1973.

28   CU, 61–63, 623–624.

29   David W. Dunlop, "Perry Watkins, 48, Gay Sergeant Won Court battle With Army," *New York Times,* March 21, 1996. 34.

30   "Loud–Mouthed Prophet," *The Monroe News-Star,* Monroe, LA; April 28, 1967. 4A.

31   Douglas Walter Bristol, editor of compilation, *Integrating the US Military* (Baltimore, MD; Johns Hopkins University Press, 2017) 99–100. (Henceforth IUSM)

32   *IBID*, 11–12, 101.

33   *IBID*, 109.

34   *IBID*, 103–104.

35   James E. Westheider, *The African American Experience in Vietnam: Brothers in Arms.* (New York, N.Y.: Rowman and Littlefield Publishers, Inc., 2007) 43-44.

36   IUSM, 104.

37   VAET, 384.

38   IUSM, 108.

39   APH, 253.

40   Clayborne Carson and David J. Garrow, Eds, *Eyes on the Prize: A Reader and Guide* (New York, N.Y.; Penguin Press, *1987)* 201–204.

41   Jerry Lembcke, *Hanoi Jane: War, Sex & Fantasies of Betrayal* (Amherst, MA: University of Massachusetts Press, 2010) 22. (Henceforth HJ)

42   Catherine Lucey, "Trump on John McCain: 'I like people who weren't captured,'" *Arizona Daily Star,* Tucson, AZ. July 19, 2015. A11.

43   John Perritano, *John McCain: An American Hero* (New York, N.Y.: Sterling Children's Books, 2018) 75-142

44   *IBID*, 145, 157.

45   John Kerry, *Every Day is Extra* (New York, N.Y.: Simon and Schuster, 2018) 52. (Henceforth EDIE)

46   *IBID,* 191.

47   *IBID*, 127, 128.

48   TVW, 480-481.

49   EDIE, 131.

50   *IBID*, 190.

51   *IBID*, 194.

52   *IBID*, 238.

53   "A New Vietnam Battle," *Des Moines Register,* Des Moines, Iowa, August 29, 2004. 4A.

54   Maria L. LaGanga, Matea Gold and Stephen Braun, "Kerry to File Complaint Tying Bush to Attack Ads," *Los Angeles Times,* August 21, 2004. A1, A10, A11.

55   *IBID*, 124–126.

56   Henry and Erika Holzer, *"Aid and Comfort": Jane Fonda in North Vietnam.* (Jefferson, N.C.: McFarland and Company, Inc., 2002.)

57   *IBID*, 62-63, 66, 75, 102.

58   *IBID*, 31.

59   Tony Norman, "Neither Forgiving nor Forgetting." *Pittsburgh Post-Gazette,* Pittsburgh, PA. April 26, 2005. A2.

60   Steve Smith, "Jane Fonda's spit–and–run assailant clearly gutless." *Los Angeles Times,* Los Angeles, CA. April 25, 2005. E3.

61   Daniel Berrigan, AI, 1990 (ca.).

62   HJ, 19.

63   "Pilots Out By Friday?," *Ithaca Journal,* Ithaca, New York. February 14, 1968. 17.

64   "Pacifists: US Fumbled," *Press and Sun-Bulletin,* Binghamton, New York, February 19, 1968. 1,9.

65   APH, 479.

66   Jim O'Grady, "Apologies, good Friends, for the Fracture of Good Order," *The Nation,* May 3, 2016. www.thenation.com

67   Harrison Smith, "Paul Booth, labor leader and antiwar activist, dies at 74," *Washington Post,* Washington, D.C. January 19, 2018.

68   Sam Roberts, "Paul Booth, Antiwar Organizer and Union Stalwart, Dies at 74," New York, N.Y. January 18, 2018.

69   Todd Gitlin, "The Mind of Paul Booth, 1943-2018," *Dissent Magazine.* January 23, 2018. www.dissentmagazine.org

70   "Wake Up America!" Spoken word album *God Bless America – Shoot Nixon,* 1970.

71   Pat Thomas, *Did It! From Yippie to Yuppie: Jerry Rubin, An American Revolutionary* (Seattle, WA. Fantagraphics Books, 2017) 40–41. (Henceforth DI)

72   John Kifner, "Hippies Shower $1 Bills on Stock Exchange Floor," *New York Times,* New York, N.Y. August 25, 1967. 23.

73   DI, 45–49.

74   *IBID*, 73–81.

75   Judy Gumbo, AI, February 2019.

76   *IBID*.

77   DI, 100–111.

78   Robert D. McFadden, "Remembering Columbia, 1968," *New York Times,* New York, N.Y. April 25, 2008.

79   Mark Rudd, AI, January 2020.

80   John Kifner, "Radicals Detect Gain in Chicago Strife," *New York Times,* New York, N.Y. October 14, 1969.

81   Rudd, AI.

82   Mark Rudd, *Underground: My Life with SDS and the Weathermen.* (New York, N.Y.: Harper Collins Publishers, 2009) 306-307. (Henceforth UML)

83   James Calhoun, *The Real Spiro Agnew: Commonsense Quotations of a Household Word* (Gretna, LA: Pelican Publishing Company, Inc., 1970) 76.

84   "Thousands in 8–Hour Parade Backing GIs," *Star-Gazette,* Elmira, N.Y. May 14, 1967. 1.

85   "It's a Banner Day for Viet Loyalty," *Daily News,* New York, N.Y. May 14, 1967. 3, 33, 56.

86   Edward Benes, "Parade Chief Says It was The Greatest," *Daily News,* New York, N.Y. May 15, 1967. 5.

87   Homer Bigart, "War Foes Here Attacked by Construction Workers," *New York Times,* May 9, 1970.

88   "Hard-Hats' Anger Boils Over Students," *Press and Sun-Bulletin,* Binghamton, New York, May 15, 1970. 1, 8A.

89   Jean Crafton and Frank Mazza, "Hard-Hats & Pickets Co-Exist," *Daily News,* New York, N.Y., May 14, 1970. 14.

90   "Workers Back President in Giant Parade," *Daily News-Journal,* Murfreesboro, Tennessee, May 21, 1970. 1, 9.

91   "150,000 marchers back Nixon in N.Y.," *Minneapolis Star,* Minneapolis, Minnesota, May 21, 1970. 4.

LIVING THE ERA

JIM SLATTERY

"Heads the Navy, tails the Air Force." Jim Slattery tossed a coin into the air and allowed that the outcome would determine his future. It came up heads…the Navy. An odd fate for a young man who could not swim very well and who lived in a town in the center of the State of Kansas. He was right square in the middle of the country and could not have possibly been more landlocked. Jim was raised near Dodge City; a town best known for being the home of famous western heroes; Wyatt Earp and Bat Masterson. He lived on a farm where his father toiled away and his mother raised eight children. When he finished high school he had no job and so thought that he'd give some time to the service of his country. After boot camp Jim learned to work in a ship's engine room. He was then assigned to a destroyer, the USS *Maddox*.

In 1964 he had been at sea for about six or seven months when the *Maddox* was ordered to the Gulf of Tonkin off the coast of North Vietnam. Jim, like millions of other Americans, had never heard of Vietnam. He "didn't even know what that place was." Soon after their arrival in the Gulf there was a boiling hot and sunny August Sunday afternoon. The part of the crew that was on duty wasn't doing anything except "tending their watches and making the ship go." Jim and his buddies were all lying underneath a gun tub trying to find some shade. Then at about four o'clock the alarm was sounded and over the loudspeaker came the orders, "All hands, man your battle stations, man your battle stations, this is no drill, man your battle stations!"

And from that point on all hell broke loose. North Vietnamese in three PT boats were attacking the *Maddox*. Jim heard the command warning over the speaker, "Stand by for torpedoes." He and his shipmates did everything they could to cause the *Maddox* to zigzag as fast as possible and succeeded in not being struck by the enemy assault. Jim felt the whole vessel shake when his ship's five-inch guns opened fire as they beat off their attackers.

On August 4th there appeared to be another encounter. This one happened late at night when the seas were rough and the only thing they could fire at were confusing images appearing on the radar screen because no one could actually see anything. There was a lot of time standing around waiting for torpedoes that would never come. The USS *Turner Joy*, also a destroyer, joined them. Jim heard their big guns blazing away as they fired blindly into the dark. He heard that they didn't stop until they literally ran out of ammunition. Concerning that night's action Jim later commented, "If you want to argue whether the Vietnamese were there or not I'm gonna say they were, but so many people say they weren't, but they weren't there and I was."

Jim believed, "They attacked us a couple of times and now they needed to be put in their place."[1] Those two reported confrontations gave LBJ the impetus that was required to gain authorization from Congress and retaliate against Vietnam. The resulting Gulf of Tonkin Resolution was the closest thing to a declaration of war that the US would issue during the Vietnam Era.

WILLIAM SIMS

In 1950 when Will was 8 his family moved to Milwaukee. His father was a foundry worker and his mother a nurse's aid. As a young African-American student he attended a segregated high school. Later he found a job making automobile frames. He tried college for a year and then dropped out and quicker than you could snap your fingers he was drafted. There were lots of people dodging the draft and otherwise resisting it but William thought, "Hey, I'll give it two years." It was the early days of America's involvement in the war and he did not imagine that he would soon be bound for the 101st Airborne Division and then Vietnam. He was sent up to the front right away, the Central Highlands. His unit stayed out in the field for weeks on end with William serving as point man on patrols. The men were transported by helicopter from LZ to LZ on search and destroy missions; find the enemy, make contact, kill them.

Sometimes on the trail he'd find leaflets left by the VC. "WHY ARE YOU HERE BLACK MAN? YOUR FIGHT IS AT HOME." He was told by his Sergeant to disregard them, just burn them up. It would take a lot more than leaflets to rattle William. He had the right attitude to deal with the perilous position of walking point. He was cool. William was the first one the enemy would see but he wasn't afraid because, after all, with his weapon in hand he was deadly.

One day just before entering into a major battle he saw some raw recruits, four African-American teenage soldiers and they were sweating profusely. William tore a green sheet from a clothesline by a hut. He handed it to the young men and ordered, "Make sweat bands." They tore the sheet up and each soldier made a band to wrap around his head.

Soon thereafter the battle was joined. A large number of Vietnamese charged hard, attacking William and his company. When the action started he was on the outside of a row of G.I.'s who were receiving heavy fire. At one point he saw a hand grenade bounce passed him and then explode close to the back of his legs. Shrapnel tore through his boots. William had a habit of tying his boots unusually tight and he was told later in the hospital that the tight boots served as a tourniquet and kept him from bleeding to death. After the blast he got up and started to fire and then he saw his Lieutenant fall wounded in the middle of the battlefield. William leapt from his foxhole, ran over and grabbed the Lieutenant by the collar, then dragged him about twenty yards, put him in a foxhole and handed him his rifle.

Just then the machine-gunner fell dead and lay across his weapon. William ran over, moved the body of his buddy, got behind the gun and commenced firing. Beside him his comrades were falling dead and wounded while in front the Vietnamese were being cut to ribbons in large numbers by William's relentless machine-gun fire. At last he was overcome by his wounds, was relieved and brought back to a medevac helicopter. While he lay on the chopper waiting for it to evacuate the battlefield he saw some of the American dead being brought to the rear and among them were the four young men, still wearing green sweat bands, an image he knew he could never forget.

As the helicopter lifted off, laden with the dead and wounded, William thought that the battle had waged on for hours. He glanced at his watch – just twenty-five minutes had passed. "Twenty-five minutes, I can't believe it," he thought. "Time is in your mind, man." He would never wear a watch again.

For his actions in that battle he was awarded a Bronze Star with a "V" for valor. He also earned an Army Commendation Medal and a Purple Heart. When he came back home he felt a lot differently then when he had first gone to Vietnam because he thought there was too much emphasis on the profits people were earning from the war. He became convinced that it was not about altruism but all about people making money.

Will learned that the Secretary of Defense Robert McNamara had lowered the standards for people to get into the military. In addition, people who were getting into trouble and facing jail time were allowed to enter the service instead of the penitentiary. He noted that McNamara reduced the standards regarding IQ as well. He thought about somebody who was mentally slow going into the service and being trained to use a weapon. "That's not too cool for nobody – especially the guy who has to be in the field with him. C'mon man." he thought. William believed it was one of those "rich people's" kind of ideas. They're going to lower the standards to protect their own kids, he thought, so they won't need to go.

Soon he returned to his old job. He found himself on the assembly line listening to the repeating sounds of the machinery and before long he began to think it was machine-gun fire and he could see, with his mind's eye, the dead Vietnamese and the dead young men with green sweatbands. The production line would slow and he found that the guys would have to tap him on the shoulder and bring him back to reality saying, "We're losing time."

He gravitated to people that had experiences similar to his own and they began to organize. Along with others William helped to establish the Veterans of the Central City, which morphed into the National Association for Black Veterans (NABVETS). They marched against the war in Washington, D.C. a number of times and they marched in a demand for treatment for Agent Orange victims. Having returned from Vietnam Will realized that his fighting had just begun.[2]

HEATHER BOOTH

Heather learned how to organize from African American Civil Rights activists. In 1964 she gained first hand experience when she went to Mississippi with the Freedom Project. A major purpose was to encourage black citizens to register to vote. Obviously this was a very dangerous proposition in 1964's Deep South. When the political establishment wouldn't let Black people register, local leaders created the Mississippi Freedom Democratic Party. When they attended the Democratic National Convention in Atlantic City the Freedom Project challenged the way elections were held. As a result of people from all over the country organizing there was a Voting Rights Act ratified within one year.

The second purpose of the Freedom Project was to help create a "freedom school." This was an arena for teaching how regular every-day people can make history. The school also taught reading and writing for those who were older and had never been to school. Heather learned more about organizing from the African-Americans that she worked with than she could have ever dreamed. She realized that the Civil Rights movement gave people the model of what individuals could do to improve society. She believed that if you organize you can change the world. She recognized that as each movement emerged in the 60's it owed its legacy in large part to the Civil Rights movement.

Heather took the skills that she developed in Mississippi back North with her. She became active in the movement against the war in Vietnam and in the budding women's movement. One night she was speaking at an SDS meeting on a college campus and one young fellow, a leader of the group, shouted out while she was in the middle of her talk, "Ah, shut up." This sort of chauvinistic disrespect was not uncommon in American society among even the more progressive young men. When she finished speaking Heather tapped each woman in the audience on the shoulder and said, "Let's go upstairs." Nearly half the organization left the meeting. Realizing that they would have to take matters into their own hands if they were going to gain the respect that they deserved they formed a group called WRAP, Women's Radical Action Program in the SDS tradition.

The group did such things as notice how many, they'd call it "significant responses," that teachers gave to women versus male students. For instance, a Professor would say, "James, what do you think about this?" and after he answered the Professor would say, "James, I think that was an interesting comment you made but have you considered this?" Then, "Robert, what did you think about this?" "Robert, that's a brilliant comment." "Steve, what do you think?" "Oh, Steve you've really done your work." Then, at last, "Mary, what do you think?" Mary would give her answer and the Professor did not react. It was typically a ratio of four to one significant responses for men versus women. So Heather and her team prepared people to go into class where they might say, "I thought that what Mary said was interesting. Can we go back to what Mary said?" Or, "Building on what Mary said, what about this?" That was one example of what they did to try to increase equality for women in the classroom.

As the decade wore on there was more and more organizing around women's concerns. And there was much to be done. Movements interconnected with one another – civil rights, student rights, anti-Vietnam war work. There was, for example, the Jeanette Rankin Brigade to follow in the tradition of Congresswomen Rankin who voted against entry into World War I and was the lone vote against entering World War II.[3]

In 1966 while at a sit-in at the University of Chicago protesting the drafting of young men into the military to fight in Vietnam, she met an energetic and highly intelligent young activist by the name of Paul Booth. He had come to the campus as an outside speaker when he was the National Secretary of SDS. After three days of the sit-in Paul asked her to marry him. (She said "yes" and they were together for the next fifty years.)[4]

The late 1960's were the first time in history that half of the college-age population of America was actually attending college and so there was the basis for an effective student movement. Heather's mother had been valedictorian of her high school and received a scholarship from Hunter College but her father wouldn't accept it because he didn't believe that women should be educated, but now there was a transformation of a woman's role in American education.[5] The times had changed. The opportunity for advancement was there and it was up to the women to take advantage of it.

Yet there were tremendous difficulties still to be faced. A friend of Heather's at the University of Chicago was raped at knifepoint in her dorm room. When she went to the student health service for a gynecological exam she was told such exams were not covered in her plan, and was given a lecture on her "promiscuity." Heather and other women sat in with her friend at the health service to change the policy. Indeed, it was changed and women, from then on, were given full gynecological coverage, careful counseling and kind support.[6]

Also, while she was in college a friend told her that his sister was pregnant, not ready to have a baby and was suicidal. His sister wanted to find someone to perform an abortion. This was at a time when if three people even talked about performing an abortion it was considered a conspiracy to commit a felony. Heather found someone who would help. The doctor had been a civil rights leader in Mississippi until his name appeared on a Ku Klux Klan death list and he moved to Chicago and opened a clinic. He performed the abortion. Then word spread and someone else called Heather and word spread some more and another young woman called. Soon she set up a system and called it "Jane." When someone called her dorm and asked for "Jane" then Heather would get on the phone. Over time she trained others to carry on because there were just so many women calling for help. They gave direction to thousands of women before the Roe v. Wade decision legalized abortion.[7]

JOHN KETWIG

John had long hair and loved to play the drums. He imagined that if he stayed with it eventually he would be discovered and become America's answer to The Beatles. When he wasn't pounding away on his drum kit his head was under the hood of an automobile, doing what he loved the most, repairing vehicles. He was eighteen, in good health, single, not in college and didn't have much money; therefore it was evident to John that he would soon be drafted. He heard that if he volunteered for three years he could choose what training he would receive in the Army. So he signed up for vehicle mechanic.

On December 30th, 1966 John reported for Basic Combat Training at Fort Dix in New Jersey. Basic proved to be far worse than he had anticipated. His particular Drill Sergeant was, for some reason, into extreme and unnecessary harassment. Sure the other Sergeants were tough, they were supposed to be, but to John's mind there was something seriously wrong with this man. For instance, one night about a foot of snow had fallen and everyone was awakened, ordered from their warm bunks, sent outside in boxer shorts and combat boots, handed dustpans and told to shovel the parking lot. Some of the guys got sick and were then put on Kitchen Police (KP) for punishment.

If a minor infraction was committed the offending recruit was ordered to dig a foxhole with an entrenching tool six feet by six feet and when you were done you had to just fill it back in. John didn't want to be there in the first place and so his resentment began to quickly build. He thought that nobody wanted to be there. Nobody wanted to be part of the whole thing. He wanted to be back at the Chevy dealership working away on cars but instead he was shoveling snow with a dustpan in his underwear. "How the heck did this happen?" he wondered.

On his birthday he was put on KP for what he thought was a "happy birthday" wish from the Drill Sergeant. While working in the officer's dining room he put salt in the sugar shakers and sugar in the saltshakers. They were just little things to be a pain in the neck, to rebel. That was the environment he was in. He began to think, "We are adversaries. It's us against them. We aren't here to do our patriotic duty or anything even like that."

When training was all said and done John was ordered to go to Vietnam. When his gigantic cargo plane landed, the back opened up and an intense wave of heat rushed in, welcoming him to Southeast Asia. He ended up transferring to another plane for his assignment in Pleiku (play-koo). And then, just like that, there he was in Vietnam. It was the rainy season and the whole base was under water. One soldier actually drowned in a huge mud puddle. The poor guy couldn't swim and got in over his head. This was definitely not a fun place to be.

They worked for 12 to 16 hours a day, whatever it took. He got tired. It got tedious. Some of the trucks that he worked on had broken down and some of them had been blown up. They could blend pieces together to make one good truck out of four wrecks.

One day, in November of 1967, the Sergeant shouted, "We need volunteers. Anybody with a drivers license." Sick and tired of the monotony of the daily routine John raised his hand and was assigned to drive one of the trucks. A convoy of about forty vehicles loaded down with desperately needed ammunition sped up the road as fast as possible. He was heading to Doc To (dock-toe) where a huge battle was raging. The road was so narrow that tree limbs were hitting the mirrors on both sides of the vehicle. The truck in front of John's was an 18-wheeler flat bed loaded to the brim with ammo. Suddenly, it ran over a landmine and there was a colossal explosion. Somehow, don't ask him how, John and his truck emerged from the smoke on the other side of that explosion. His windshield was smashed and everything was covered with mud but he managed to maneuver around the crater caused by the huge blast. The truck that was in front of him, along with its driver, had been blown to smithereens but John and the rest of the convoy pressed onward.

At last, they stopped and began to distribute their life saving (and taking) cargo. As the battle raged on around him mortars were pouring in like mad. While unloading the truck and standing in knee-deep mud he once again had to stop and ask himself, "How the heck did this happen?!"

When he was finally back at the base John thought himself lucky just to be in one piece.

While he was in Vietnam a lot of people were killed in bombings, both soldiers and civilians. It troubled John to see so many die horribly from napalm, white phosphorous and cluster bombs with shredded plastic pellets undetectable on X-Rays. The cruelty of the whole thing was absolutely beyond anything he could have imagined. In addition, after a while he became cynical because he learned that he couldn't trust anyone. For example, the South Vietnamese Army had a draft. John and his buddies raised three hundred dollars to pay to the Vietnamese draft board and thereby keep their favorite Vietnamese barber from going into the Army. One night, soon thereafter, the very same barber slipped in under the fence with a handful of fellow VC. He was shot dead in the barbed wire holding a satchel of bombs to blow up the same GI's, including John, who thought he was their friend.

The Tet Offensive was a great psychological defeat for John and his comrades. They had been told over and over that they were winning and that "the light at the end of tunnel" was getting brighter and brighter. But then suddenly one night the enemy was in every town, everywhere. John could see the glow of flames from Pleiku burning in the darkness of the night and all the helicopters hovering over and he could hear the seemingly endless shooting; he was terrified. That night he really doubted that he would ever make it home again.

During Tet the enemy had lists of names and went from house to house looking for people who had worked for or cooperated with the Americans. Once identified they raped, otherwise assaulted or killed these people. There was an old man, about 70 years old, who was the "shit burner" for the camp. He dragged out 55-gallon drums everyday and threw it in a pit and burned the "crap." He was a jovial little old man, grateful to have some money coming in and John and his buddies all got along with him. Everyone thought he was just a joy. The VC went to his house and raped and shot his daughter and his wife and held him down and shot each of his arms and each of his legs. Some time later somebody brought him out to the camp to say, "hello." To John the sight of the old man could only be described as pathetic, just as horrible a thing as you could possibly see. The old fellow was left a total invalid and there wasn't much for an invalid to do in Vietnam to earn a living.

John knew that if he survived there for 365 days there would be a plane waiting to take him out and life would go back to making sense again but that seemed very far off a lot of the time. When the 365th day finally came his Vietnam experience at last began to draw to a conclusion. He did not want to go back to the "World," as GI's referred to the US, and stand on the steps of the Pentagon with the protesters, even though he agreed with them. He knew he'd get into trouble if he went back and so he asked to be transferred to Thailand where he spent the next year there trying to make sense of the insanity he witnessed in Vietnam. In retrospect he asked himself, "How the heck did that happen?"[8]

BILL LANE

Bill waited with what can only be described as great anticipation to go to Vietnam. He was one of America's elite Green Berets and he was itching to get into the action. However, regulations clearly stated that brothers couldn't be in a combat zone at the same time. His brother, a Marine, was serving out his tour of duty. And so at almost the same minute that Bill's brother's plane left Vietnamese air space Bill's plane headed in the opposite direction and right into the war.[9]

His role was that of an advisor to the South Vietnamese Army (ARVN) and as such he took command as Executive Officer of a unit. He marveled sometimes at the heroics of his soldiers and he would think, "They're braver than me." But other times he was disgusted by some of the soldier's lack of interest in the effort. Many didn't take the war seriously at all.[10]

Shortly after his arrival his unit was attacked during the Tet Offensive. He was pinned down overnight, taking shelter behind tombstones in a Buddhist cemetery. But Bill relished the action, which occurred often enough. He believed that combat helped him to become a real man and he was flooded with self-confidence. Following his unit's victory over the North Vietnamese regiment that invaded their area he felt exhilaration brought about by extreme fatigue. How he and his comrades then all cursed when the *New York Times* clippings arrived claiming they had actually been defeated.

Bill found that even through all of the violence and hatred that he didn't lose his humanity. Later on he would write, "I can still see the terror in the eyes of the North Vietnamese prisoners brought before me. I was the first American they had ever seen, tall and blond (then), and undoubtedly going to kill them. They nearly collapsed in relief when I handed each of them a few of cigarettes and told them: 'no sweat.'"[11]

Although he relished the action of combat a good part of his time was spent just waiting and waiting. His main mission was to ambush the enemy. His unit would hide in the foothills as the Vietcong came down from the mountains to recruit people. Often they would intercept them but the clever VC would just as often elude their ambush. He couldn't help, in the quiet times, but think just how beautiful Vietnam was and how grand it would be to return one day in peaceful times and sit with old friends and sip a beer or two. Yes, he thought, he would love to do just that.

When his tour of duty was over Bill considered volunteering for another tour but decided not to push his luck and so returned home. He came back to a nation divided. He couldn't understand why the people weren't more supportive of the soldiers and the conflict. He thought that it was a noble war and that the cause was just. Godless communism, he believed, could not be allowed to spread! He was very disappointed in the behavior of some of the American people and positively despised the ones that were carrying and waving North Vietnamese flags. He considered them to be nothing more than traitors.[12]

Bill thought the politicians played the most important roles because they made all of the decisions. He felt that they should have decided to make a full-scale invasion of North Vietnam and if it were up to him he would have given the okay and join in on the charge.

Bill found it embarrassing and hated it when he saw a veteran feeling sorry for himself. He thought Hollywood movies were portraying the American soldier in Vietnam as "racist, neurotic, drug crazed, feral, a hopeless pawn of a rotten society sent to fight an unjust war." And he detested it. He despised veterans that whined, acted "nutty" and looked for a free ride. He thought they shamed themselves compared with say World War II vets. Bill refused to believe in support groups or posttraumatic stress disorder (PTSD) or the consequences of exposure to Agent Orange.[13]

Mary Kambic

It was not easy for Mary to be against the war and march in rallies and speak out when her father, Colonel A. Kevin Quinn, whom she greatly admired, was a hero of the Second World War. Yet her religious convictions were strong and she had to do what she believed to be right, just as she had been taught. Mary had a heritage of a powerful connection with the Catholic Church. Her father and his five brothers all entered the seminary at one time or another. Three became priests and one of them was actually a chaplain that ministered to the Marines at the battle of Iwo Jima in World War II.[14]

Her father told Mary how he and his men, when liberating a concentration camp, searched for Martin Niemoller, the Evangelical Minister who wrote, "First they came for the Socialists, and I did not speak out— Because I was not a Socialist. Then they came for the Trade Unionists, and I did not speak out— Because I was not a Trade Unionist. Then they came for the Jews, and I did not speak out— Because I was not a Jew. Then they came for me—and there was no one left to speak for me."

Her father taught Mary about ethics and war. For example, he was proud to be among the very first American Officers to enter the concentration camp at Dachau to liberate the inmates. Also, he taught her that although war may be a necessary evil at times there are boundaries that must be respected. For example, he told her that if he were ordered to harm civilians he would refuse. In her estimation, Vietnam stepped beyond the "boundaries that must be respected" and, therefore, she must speak out.

Her mom was very active politically. As soon as the Irish-born immigrant achieved citizenship she became a Democratic Committeewoman. There were only four people in Mary's entire town that were Democrats; her father, her mother and two reporters from the *New York Times*. Her mother's political activism rubbed off on Mary and at 12 years old, she campaigned for JFK. Her mother had her on the street handing out buttons and campaign literature. In addition, there were some very progressive journals to which Mary's mother subscribed. So that when she was a teenager she was reading all about Father Daniel Berrigan.

Later on, when Mary's 19-year-old cousin was killed in Vietnam, apparently by friendly fire, her disillusionment with the war grew more intense. Now a rift began to develop in the family. Her sister, for example, worked for the military and was very committed to them. In addition to her cousin's death, people like Father Berrigan really convinced her to take a strong antiwar stance. She invited the radical Priest to speak at her college in 1966. It was interesting to her because some people were having a fit over his appearance and she couldn't even find a place for him to stay. She was in a dormitory so the best she could do was arrange for him to stay at a nearby hotel. A couple of years later the situation had changed significantly. Berrigan came back and people were falling all over themselves to accommodate the now-famous political activist and theological intellectual.

Mary planned to go to Washington to demonstrate in a major protest. Before she left her father asked her not to march on the Pentagon. He had a top-secret clearance and he was still in the Army Reserves and so he said that he was going to ask that she not go to the military's national headquarters because knowledge of her presence could put him in a difficult position. She marched in the demonstration but when she approached the bridge that led to the Pentagon she didn't cross because she had given her father her word.

The scariest thing that happened to her during the era was when she was arrested with 80 students following pacifist and antiwar activist Dave Dellinger (also a Chicago 8 alumnus), coming to the University of Pittsburgh. They were sitting around at a reception at a Professor's apartment when the place was raided. The police said that they found dangerous drugs when in actuality it was the Professor's cold and sinus medications. Nonetheless, everyone was dragged off to the police station. One man who had been in a concentration camp came to secure the release of his son. He could hardly speak because he was so upset, but managed to shout to the police, "You are like the Gestapo!"

Mary was soon in for another shock when on the next day the headlines in the local paper read, "80 Students Arrested In Drug Raid." Mary was not prepared for that at all and she plainly could not believe what happened to her and the other students. She was a good student who obeyed the rules; she was not the type the police were describing in their courtroom statements. Yet she along with everyone else was convicted of disorderly conduct. Mary was hurt by the reaction in her school and the community when people literally turned their back on her and her companions, or they would just be iced out. They weren't taking drugs or anything but that was the image she and all the rest were tagged with. Then a local liberal newspaper came out with an editorial that said it was really wrong to do this to all these young people and some finally began to come around and believe them.

Mary didn't graduate on time because in her senior year Dr. Martin Luther King was assassinated. School would have to wait; she felt a sense of urgency, to carry on King's efforts and devote herself fully to the antiwar movement.[15]

JOSE FLORES

Until he was 12 years old he was raised in Puerto Rico, in the countryside where his grandfather was a farmer and his uncle raised pigs. Jose loved the outdoors and he loved farm life but then his parents had to move to the hustling and bustling urban New York City for work. Jose's dad was a mechanic and his mother worked in a factory and so before long he transformed, as he had to, into a typical city kid from a blue-collar household.

His family had a long tradition of serving in the Army. Unlike other young people that he knew, Jose didn't want to join the military to run away from anything but instead wanted to do it because he believed it was his duty as an American citizen. At 18 he volunteered right out of high school for three years of service, then requested an infantry assignment and discovered that there was no problem getting it, because after all, it was October 1968 and young folks who were ready to fight were very much in demand. Jose trained at Fort Jackson in South Carolina and from there went directly to Vietnam.

When he first arrived he was given about five days of training and was briefed on what area his unit covered. Then without any further ado he started to venture out into the field. Jose along with his squad would go out for a day or two. A helicopter outside the base would transport them up or they'd walk. Every soldier would have a hundred rounds of M-60 machine-gun bullets plus ten magazines for their own M-16 rifle and a couple of hand grenades.

Typically his squad's assignment would be to go out a "few klick's" (kilometers) and set up an ambush for the night. They were involved in a couple of really intense firefights where he and his buddies killed twenty or twenty-five Vietcong. An average firefight, however, might last ten to twenty minutes, resulting in but a handful of "Killed in Action" (KIA's). Once it was over they'd pick up and move out just in case the enemy had more people in the rear. He saw his share of Americans killed and wounded but his unit didn't experience more casualties than most.

Usually the enemy traveled in small numbers, maybe six or eight people. A few times, however, Jose's unit was attacked at his base by a massive amount of enemy soldiers. The next day following one of those large attacks they went out and, finding bodies everywhere, they buried them all together in a huge crater, pushing the lifeless forms in with a noisy old steam shovel.

He was involved in firefights where he saw people that looked way too young to be in combat. He saw the dead ones up close and personal and some looked to him like they were children. They were wearing civilian clothes or sometimes they had on black pajamas.

Another one of his jobs was to help keep the local village safe from the Vietcong. Sometimes they had to stay among the people because the VC would come in at night and steal food and try to find out who was in charge and torture them for information about the Americans.

In time Jose worked his way up from private to buck Sergeant. He had positive experiences with many of the Vietnamese people but his biggest problem was that he just couldn't trust anyone. They might be friendly talking to him during the day but at night they might be VC. He'd go into a home and he'd move a piece of furniture and there would be a tunnel used by the enemy to come in. He came across that a lot. One of the guy's in his squad had the job of going down into those tunnels. He was the shortest one and so fit in fairly easily. He would go down there with a .45 and a flashlight and be gone for a while. Sometimes he'd meet the enemy and it was definitely kill or be killed. He killed. After they were secured Jose climbed down into the tunnels to see what they were like and what he saw amazed him. They seemed to go on forever under the village, under the Post and deep into the woods. Some had rooms like a hospital or a conference room in which to plan attacks.

When Jose had time to appreciate his surroundings he thought that Vietnam was so appealing it reminded him of his early childhood in rural Puerto Rico. He would sometimes say to himself, "What a shame we are here for a war in such a beautiful country."

Jose thought that the South Vietnamese soldiers could only be described as horrible. He could not trust them because the minute a firefight started some of them would just turn around and run. Sometimes they were supposed to accompany his squad and he could plainly see that they had no intention of being out there in combat with them, none.

Jose would never drink alcohol or take drugs especially after he heard of a place called the Black Virgin Mountain. Some of the guys there had hard booze and a lot of beer and they got drunk. Then the VC charged and overran the base. That wasn't going to happen to his base.

He was impressed with the NVA and thought they were professional soldiers, they were good soldiers. He didn't think that the Vietcong were but he thought they were dedicated to their cause. He saw it as they were defending their neighborhood, like he would have done back in New York. After a while he estimated that casualties ran 4 to 1, four dead NVA or VC to every American killed. But even still the body counts would be greatly exaggerated. Sometimes he'd get into a firefight and the report would say they killed thirty VC and Jose knew that they might have killed five.

Often the enemy would take back land that Jose's unit won only a few weeks before. That happened to them a lot. They'd take a village where the VC were hiding out and maybe a couple of GIs would be wounded or killed and a month later the higher-ups wanted them to go back again because the VC had returned. Americans weren't holding any land and according to Jose, "That pissed a lot of guys off."[16]

MICHAEL SMAR

Michael was highly intelligent and never failed to do a great job in school. He, along with his friends, were well read; especially when it came to current events. By the time they graduated from high school in 1967 they had given a lot of thought and spent hours in discussion concerning the war raging away in Vietnam. Michael came to the conclusion that the war was pointless and saw absolutely no merit in the so-called "Domino Theory." He believed that many of the people that were being killed were innocent pawns between the Communists and their own government. His conscience would not allow him to carry a gun into this sort of conflict.

On the other hand, he did possess a strong sense of duty to his fellow countrymen who were being killed and wounded by the score each and every day. He applied for and received 1AO status in the draft. This was the equivalent of 1A, he was qualified to serve but was designated an objector. In short he would still enter the service but not carry a weapon. And so it was that following graduation from high school at the end of May he found himself in the Army by the fourth of July.

Michael was trained in a company of Seventh Day Adventists. Although he was not of that faith he learned all about the non-violent values of the religion. They formed a great group dedicated to learning first aid and saving lives. He trained for six months in San Antonio, Texas and by the end of the training he was able to do everything from taking care of a sucking chest wound to delivering a baby.

When he finished with corpsman school he was whisked away to Vietnam. As his plane flew lower and lower he could see the Vietnamese people below, wearing their conical hats while bent over and tending to their rice paddies. Ultimately, Michael helicoptered into his new basecamp somewhere around Loc Minh (lock- min). The chopper landed in a small clearing of a wooded area and he was quickly introduced to the other four medics that were stationed with this infantry company. Desperate for help they were more than happy to see him and he was welcomed with open arms.

Word spread among some of the soldiers that the Vietcong and North Vietnamese regulars were preparing for a big attack. It was all pretty amazing to Michael because it seemed that it was just one minute ago that he was blissfully studying in his high school classroom and the next he was standing in the jungle waiting for God-knows-what to happen. He took it all in his stride and within a couple of days he was off with the infantry division, on a mission, marching in staggered single file through the woods and through the seemingly peaceful little villages. At night the soldiers would set up a small base camp and wait for the VC or the NVA to come their way. While out on a mission he couldn't help but observe the beauty of the country, the hills and the valleys, the sun on the rice paddies, the smell of the incense burning in the villages. It was a lovely place.

However, he didn't have to wait long for the peaceful scene to be transformed into an arena of death; because by early February the Tet Offensive was in full swing. Many of Michael's comrades were killed or wounded in frequent and intense firefights. The other Medics were wounded in such a way that within a few short months by the end of the offensive Michael found himself at 18 years old to be the senior medic of the outfit with two or three young replacements to help him with his medical chores. His fellow GIs were pleased that he didn't carry a weapon because they could be certain that he had nothing else to do but take care of them. They knew if they got shot he wasn't fiddling around with a grenade launcher or clearing a jammed M-16 but that he was trying to get to them. Michael found himself to be highly respected.

Much of what he was doing was getting people out of the line of fire. Some were already dead when he got there but he managed to save a good number of the wounded.

One day while marching through the woods the soldier in front of him was suddenly shot through the head and instantaneously killed. Michael was able to fall into a little ditch that was full of water and deep enough to provide cover. He could see the tracer bullets ricocheting right in front of him. The soldier in back of him was shot in the leg and was screaming to high heaven. One of the Sergeants was able to jump up on top of a bunker from which most of the shots were being fired and heave a hand grenade right in on top of the Vietcong and kill all in there. Michael heard the Sergeant shouting, "I got 'em! I got 'em!"

Michael leaped up out of the ditch and got to the soldier that was screaming. He saw his leg had turned 180 degrees the wrong way. Michael was able to pick him up and run a short distance, then throw him into a ditch to get him out of the line of fire. The poor guy was screaming bloody murder at the time but Michael was able to stabilize the leg. Several other members of the company were shot that day and he was able to get them to a position where he could call in the helicopters to take them to the hospital. For his bravery Michael earned a medal, the Bronze Star.

Soon after that battle his entire Company was helicoptered into the middle of nowhere to look for VC. When the choppers left them they stood in pitch darkness and proceeded to march deeper and deeper into the jungle for several miles before setting up camp at last. All he could see in the distance was the silhouette of a couple of palm trees and the lights of fireflies busily flickering in the night. He held his hand in front of his face and could just barely make it out. So there they were about 9 or 10 o'clock at night as they sat and waited and waited and waited … in dead silence.

Suddenly, at 3 in the morning there sounded a series of explosions and rapid fire that lasted only a few seconds and, just as suddenly as it had started, all was quiet once again. A moment later Michael heard from out of the pitch black someone yell, "Get the medic, get the medic!" He began to crawl over to the place where the explosions had occurred and all the bullets had been fired and he was crawling and feeling and finally his arm and his hand came up to touch bodies. All five men at that position were dead, except for one. Michael whispered, "What happened here?" and the young soldier responded with a dying voice, "We didn't see anything." All those men at that position were riddled with bullets and were like chop meat and dead as a doorknob. There was no one to save there. He realized this is Vietnam. Often you didn't see anybody, you didn't see anything, you just had death.

Once, looking out about seven or eight miles from his basecamp Michael could see the explosions caused by 500-pound bombs raining down from American B-52 airplanes. The ground around him shook and red dust rose to cover his eyes and nose but off in the distance he could make out the bright glow from the explosions. The next day they marched there and he witnessed a sight that was like something out of Dante's Inferno; entire huge trees were uprooted and turned upside down, craters in the ground twenty or thirty feet deep with nothing but mud all over the place, human bodies everywhere, including some strewn, in horribly grotesque positions, about in the trees. He had never before seen anything quiet so surreal.

After a year he was supposed to be deployed back to the States but he would have no part of that. He volunteered to stay an extra six months to work at the 24th Evacuation Hospital, a clearinghouse for all of Vietnam, in Long Binh (long-bin) a suburb of Saigon. After what he had been through, it was almost like a vacation. Food, showers, clean uniforms. It was wonderful! And then the bubble burst when a second major offensive came along. He was a corpsman in a Quonset hut emergency room and the casualties would come in by chopper to the nearby helicopter pad. The Medics would go and collect the wounded on stretchers and bring them in and line them up side by side along the length of the hut.

The surgeon would come by and inspect the wounded and tell the corpsman what to do. This one would have to get a chest x-ray right away.

This one would have to get an artery clamped. This one would have to have a chest tube placed. Prep this one to have his leg cut off. This one would have to go to the operating room right away. This one would have to be put off to the side because he was shot through the head and he'd be dead within an hour or two and let him breath his last over in the corner.

There were people in that Quonset hut lined up day and night. The helicopters were in and out non-stop. They had wounded and dying lined up all around the helicopter pad, up the street, down the street, around the block and it was just one wounded GI after another. One time when a helicopter arrived it was so full of dead and wounded that when Michael opened the door to the chopper everybody just fell out pell-mell right onto the tarmac. So they had to pick out the dead from the living and take out the ones that were still salvageable into the Quonset hut.

All the doctors, nurses and medics were dedicated to saving lives and they did an excellent job. The surgeons that he worked side by side with were some of the finest people he ever met or ever would meet and so inspired him that he had in mind to become a doctor himself one day.

And so that six months came and went. He met his father once in Vietnam. He was a captain in the Merchant Marines and he wrote Michael a letter saying that he was coming into Saigon and could he meet him there. He was able to get some time off to go visit his father when he came in on his ship to deliver his cargo. Michael thought, "This is weird.", but his father told him he would be able to get him a job when he finished his Vietnam experience. Michael was discharged in Saigon and was able to sign onto a ship that was part of a marine company. He got his papers to be an able-bodied seaman and was able to do his Merchant Marine job for a year after he got out of Vietnam. It was a great way to save his sanity and to go and see the world and make some money at the same time. He didn't want to be wrapped up in all the protests and all the stuff that was going on in the United States – even though he was agreeing more with the protesters than they could ever have imagined.[17]

PAT O'LEARY

"Get up! Get up! Get up, get up, get up! Ya gotta take the test." Pat's mother stood over his bed; fists rolled up in a ball and planted firmly on her hips, her Irish face red with anger. "Ma, I don't wanna be a cop.

Leave me alone. Leave me alone." But she would have none of it. "You get out of that bed right now." So with great reluctance he rose, got dressed and dragged himself down to the train station. He thought he'd find some place to lay low for the day and then go home and tell his mother that he took the entrance exam for the NYPD. When Pat arrived at the station he was surprised to see about thirty guys waiting and he knew every last one of them. "Where the flip are you guys going?" They were all heading out to take the test and so he rode along with them and took the test too.

Not long after that he learned that he was accepted into the police trainee unit in Brooklyn. He would not become a full-fledged policeman until he was 21 and that was still two long years away. He fast became bored with being a trainee. Pat thought it was stupid and he thought it wasn't any real police training – it was switchboard operator, gopher and mundane things like that. He really wasn't learning anything, just marking time. His brother was in Vietnam, his father had been a combat medic in World War II and a veteran of the D-Day invasion and his grandmother and grandfather were both World War I veterans. In addition, he had a Great Uncle that was killed in World War I. He began to think that maybe it was his duty to join. Maybe it was in his blood.

Pat decided to go down to the draft board and say, "I want you to cancel my police department deferment and I want to push up my draft." He was supportive of the war effort and he believed in the whole "domino theory" and stopping the spread of communism and how important that would be. For a kid who grew up in the Cold War it was like, at least in his mind, going to fight the Russians. Communism was Russia and China not these "poor little Vietnamese people" that he found when he got over there. He simply believed that what America was doing was the right thing.

It started out with one of his heroes, Eisenhower, and then it went into the next "huge gigantic" hero of his life JFK and these men were all kind of pro-war and Pat thought, "They can't be wrong can they? Could Ike be wrong? Could Kennedy be wrong? No flipping way." He joined the Army in June of 1968 and was assigned to the 101st Airborne Division and was ecstatic because he knew of the glorious history of the 101st. He was stationed in the north near the Demilitarized Zone (DMZ) and not at all far from Laos. All he found there were mountains and jungles and the occasional small village. Their job was to interdict on the Ho Chi Minh trail and keep as many men and supplies from trickling down to Saigon as was possible. Unbeknownst to the people back home they would even go back and forth across the border into Laos.

When Pat first arrived in Vietnam around Thanksgiving he reported for duty at Firebase "Birmingham." He hadn't even gotten to his bunker yet when a soldier presented him with his weapon. So on his first day with the company he became the new machine-gunner. What happens when you carry the machine gun is that as soon as the first bullet is fired the guy up front yells, "Get the gun up here!" and Pat would run up to the front and right into the heat of the action. He'd run straight down a trail to the front of the line where the ambush was taking place with bullets flying all around him and he'd get the machine gun up to start putting out a field of fire. That was the most dangerous job to have at that particular moment. The platoon tramped around through the jungles searching for and then assaulting the enemy. After about three weeks they were so cruddy and rotten and disgusting they were brought back into the firebase to clean up and resupply.

One of the worst feelings Pat had of being in combat in Vietnam was never having a front line. Just spending the whole time being surrounded. They were behind enemy lines at all times. He didn't know if they were going to be attacked from the front, the rear, the left or the right.

After sundown they'd set up a Night Defensive Position (NDP) on a hilltop where each soldier would dig a foxhole, clear a field of fire and put claymore mines out. Then get into the hole for the night. That was the last thing they did right before it started getting incredibly dark. He literally couldn't see his hand in front of his face in the jungle canopy where it was basically just pitch black and the moonlight or the stars never even showed through. Pat was in what they called a free-fire zone so his hands were never cuffed. Anything he saw that moved or sneezed was considered enemy and he'd open fire. This was not like down in Saigon or in Hue (way) where there was a contact-first situation and the Americans had to be attacked before they could fire.

There in the jungle they'd just wait until the enemy walked into their field of fire and then they'd open up on them. What followed was about maybe eight, nine, ten minutes of sheer madness. Then they'd have to sit there and hope nobody came back and attacked them with a larger force. Occasionally they'd face what they called a "big shit storm." One bad one in particular was at a river crossing. If it were any other time he'd just wish he had a fly rod and go fishing because it was so pleasant. Instead a couple of trackers and a couple of dogs were sent out to find an enemy position. Pat hated it when the dogs came out because he knew eventually something was going to happen, because the dogs were so good at finding what they were looking for and so they always led them right to where the enemy was. Suddenly all hell broke loose. Both dogs were killed, both the handlers were killed and a lot of Pat's buddies were wounded or killed. It was really a bad day for them because they didn't have much of a body count and yet they got shot up but good.

One thing Pat learned for sure was to never get drunk or high. One night while his squad was out in the jungle some of the guys back at the firebase got ahold of some booze and pot. Knowing, through their spies, the condition of many of the men, a sapper battalion attacked the base. Sappers were VC that were basically naked in a diaper and carrying satchels filled with explosives. They blew up artillery pieces and then were followed by regular troops with AK 47 rifles. A lot of Americans were killed. Miles away Pat and his squad were asleep in their foxholes on a jungle hilltop. One by one everybody started alerting each other and they could see all the tracers and all the firing that was going on far down below. Pat thought, "Oh my god, this is one big shit storm!" Then gradually they could hear over the radio the desperate pleas for help. But they had been taken by helicopter to their location and were a day and a half march away and they couldn't be found by helicopter at night. They could only watch and feel the pain of their comrades being cut to pieces.

Then for the first and only time Pat saw Puff the Magic Dragon. Puff was an incredibly heavily armed Fixed Wing C-130. It began circling around the firebase for as long as it could on fuel and presented the show of all shows. Pat had never seen anything like it before or since. It had four Gatling style mini-guns and twenty-millimeter cannon and rockets and it was firing everything it had all at once. Pat thought, "Holy crap, how could anything survive any of that?" That basically broke the attack and then from that point on they just waited for dawn to come and they all moved back towards the firebase to help out. When they arrived there were dozens and dozens of dead people, both American and Vietnamese, scattered everywhere.

After that Pat began to think of himself and his buddies as nothing but bait. Walking through the jungle trying to attract the enemy. The only thing that was going to happen was "we're gonna kill them in an ambush or they're gonna kill us in an ambush." He wrote a letter home where he told his folks that he felt like the British, the Redcoats, walking through the countryside and American colonists are hiding behind the trees just shooting at them. He thought this must be exactly what the Redcoats felt like.

As time went on the situation began to grow more surreal. One night they had an NDP set up and an elephant came crashing through the jungle. At first they didn't know what it was. "Barroom, barroom, barroom." and everybody's on the radio shouting, "What going on?!" Then the elephant tripped a flair and let out a tremendous roar. Panic stricken, the huge creature turned around and blasted back through the jungle. Pat wondered the next day, "Did I dream that? Did that really happen?"

The body count became a joke. If a company commander reported a high body count then he was heaped with praise by the higher-ups and so the number of KIA's was greatly exaggerated. If they had three KIA's it might be reported as thirty, for instance and sometimes hundreds were reported as having been killed. Based on his experience Pat knew this was ridiculous because if you were downwind for ten miles of that many dead people you'd just gag and vomit for ten days until the bodies were so decomposed they wouldn't stink anymore. He knew that when you kill somebody it would be just a matter of hours before they started to decompose and smell. In a matter of seconds, thirty seconds to a minute, they were covered with a million flies and the flies just went to work and the bodies would start to stink and rot and it was horrible, horrible, horrible. Pat knew that the whole body-count thing was just plain dumb.

Pat's fight in the jungle mountains was a lot different from what the guys in the Mekong Delta faced. Down there they could be walking across a rice paddy and look over a shoulder and see a thousand yards away just as flat as a pancake. They could easily see six or seven VC carrying AK47's and wearing black pajamas. Pat, on the other hand, couldn't see ten feet away.

As the months passed Pat became aware that if he could hang on a little longer he might just make it out of there and go home alive and in one piece. But he would never even talk about being a "short timer" until he got to about ninety days away from being sent back home. Sometimes new guys would come into Vietnam with no experience at all, just out of training and would be sitting out in a foxhole that night next to a guy that had two months left and the "short timer" would say, "If you mess anything up I'll kill you." When Pat became the squad leader he had just three months left to go. The new platoon leader appeared to Pat like he was about 16 years old when one day he told Pat, "Recon to the top of this ridge and tell me if it's a good spot for an LZ." Pat told him that it was a maneuver for an entire platoon not just a squad. He knew that if he's up there a thousand yards and gets hit they won't have time to get there before his squad was wiped out. "No, no, no we'll get there." the young lieutenant promised.

Pat got his guys together and they marched off. They went about 200 yards, which in the jungle is like two miles. He said, "Listen, we're not going to the top of this ridge line we're going to hang out here for about an hour maybe two. I'm gonna call the Lieutenant and tell him its not a good spot for an LZ. You got a problem with that?" and they all responded, "No and thank you." After an hour he called in, "We're at the top of this ridge line and it's a really terrible place for a landing zone, lots of boulders." He didn't even give him a chance to answer and he said, "We'll be back in an hour and a half. Out." They returned and no one ever said a thing about the deception.

For Pat it wasn't when he was in the fighting but rather when he was not in the fighting that was the worst. It was when he was anticipating. Because the fighting is blinding, it's deafening, it's so loud and it smells, it stinks, the cordite, the blood, the bodies. When he looked back after a fight it was like a dream, it was so bizarre. Did that really happen? Like the elephant, did that really happen? Did he really see that guy's head get blown off? Stuff like that. But then during the period of time when nothing was happening is when his nerves just frayed because he was waiting, anticipating and then he'd start getting jumpy and then tie that in with getting short. That was the big part of the anticipation – that nerve-fraying thing that happens just keeps increasing. He felt like that until the very minute that he went home.[18] Back in New York he rejoined the NYPD; a position that seemed quite safe compared to the jungles of the Ho Chi Minh Trail.

BILLY X. JENNINGS

Huey Newton   Billy

His dad was a Navy man and so Billy (right) was raised on military bases. For as long as he could remember he wished not to have anything to do with military life. He didn't like the idea of going into the service one bit because he didn't relish the thought of someone yelling at him all day long telling him what he could and could not do. His most fervent wish was to have zero to do with military life. As time went on he began to release his pent-up anger and frustrations through fighting. He'd fight anyone over anything. One day he was approached by one of his high school's Physical Ed teachers, Tommie Smith, who counseled him, "Bill, I saw you fighting and you have to take it easy. You have to choose your battles." The advice and attention was exactly what he needed and so he began to change and refocus his energies on his studies. (A few years later Billy would see Smith on television after he had chosen his own battle. After winning Olympic gold in Mexico City Smith offered, in protest, the black power salute of a raised fist in a black leather glove during the playing of the National Anthem.)

On the day he graduated from high school a considerate teacher, "a wise lady," presented him with the gift of a book; *The Autobiography of Malcolm X*. That night he boarded a Greyhound bus, cracked open the tome and headed for Oakland, California. Oakland, a large city, seemed to be a good place to distance oneself from the looming draft board.

That summer Billy took a course at Laney College. While sitting in his 11 o'clock class minding his own business he could hear the sound of chanting and oration echoing through the halls and emanating from nearby outside. A clarion call drew him to it as soon as class was dismissed. He strode to the source of the action and there he witnessed something he had never before seen; an interracial rally. He saw protest marches on TV but never anything quite like this. Black, white and Asian together as equals, as brothers and sisters and all calling for the release of Huey Newton from jail. "Free Huey! Free Huey! Free Huey!" Others were presenting fiery speeches against involvement in the Vietnam War and black oppression in America. The orators were expressing some of the same sentiments that he read about in the book about Malcolm X. The book seemed to come to life before his eyes. Some of the speakers were from the Black Panther Party and before he knew it he joined up. Then it was on. It was the summer of '68 and Billy was 17.

He took to the communal and idealistic lifestyle of the Panthers. They encouraged him to be proud of who he was. He knew for sure now that he didn't have to go to Vietnam to prove to white America that he was a man. ("You don't have to show them shit.") He already knew he was a man and if others didn't realize it then it was their problem. Black people struggled to vote in this country and so why were they supposed to be fighting for Vietnamese democracy when the fight should be "right here at home?" He believed that America was an imperialistic government and the Vietnamese were fighting for their freedom. He reasoned that African-Americans were living as a colonial people in their own country.

Before long Huey was released from jail and Billy became a personal aide to Newton himself. He found Huey to be "a dedicated and very intelligent brother." To Billy, Huey was courageous and he formed a friendship with him and his family.

When Billy was brought to court for resisting the draft the Panthers provided him with a counselor. At first he had no idea who Dr. Benjamin Spock was but soon learned he was none other than the famous pediatrician of the baby-boom generation and an important political activist. With his guidance and because of some very serious privacy violations by the federal government inflicted on Billy he was able to successfully resist military service.

During his time with the Panthers other big celebrities stepped up to help the cause including, among others, Marlon Brando, Leonard Bernstein, Candice Bergen, Jane Fonda and Donald Sutherland. Huey Newton influenced television producer Norman Lear to create a program wherein black people were depicted as well off. Lear then created *The Jeffersons*; the black family that moved on up to the Eastside and lived in a "deluxe apartment in the sky." In addition, the Panther movement caught fire around the world. Branches were formed in New Zealand, Australia, London, Israel and China among other places.

Some of the Panthers that Billy knew were recent returnees from Vietnam. They were hardened combat veterans of 21 and 22 years old. Some of these young men took the lead in seeking violent revenge and wanted to fully employ a military viewpoint to the Black Panthers. Billy personally believed it would be better in the long run to focus their energy on solving some of the many social concerns.

The Black Panther Party had just popped up as a reaction to police brutality and now they introduced programs for which much of the rest of the nation was not yet ready; free breakfast for children before school, recycling programs, escorts for senior citizens cashing their Social Security checks, a police substation in the neighborhood, testing for Sickle Cell Anemia, transportation to and from the penitentiary to help families visit incarcerated loved ones and, perhaps most importantly, registering thousands of black people to vote. The Party grew in leaps and bounds.

Over time, however, Billy saw the organization begin to falter due to differences at the leadership level, FBI sabotage and financial difficulties.[19]

MARK RUDD

Mark was an undergraduate student at Columbia University where he and his comrades had spent the last three years politicizing the campus. They had done it in any number of ways including teach-ins, sit-ins, marches, speeches and writings. At long last the consciousness of the campus was indeed raised and many students were prepared to do just about anything to help to end the war and advance the cause of racial justice. And so it was that on a day late in April 1968 Mark, along with the other leaders of the movement, Students Afro-American Society and the black community of Harlem, led the largely improvisational act of taking over five Administration buildings on campus – including one housing the office of the University's President. What followed was a week of occupation of the buildings by hundreds of students and other activists ending in brutal beatings and 720 arrests by nearly one thousand cops.[20] Assaults upon the police included over a dozen injured and one resulting in the permanent disabling of an officer.[21]

One would never have guessed that Mark would be the type to help orchestrate such radical confrontations. After all, he was a smart young man that came from a decent law-abiding family in a good neighborhood in suburban New Jersey.[22] As the campus boiled over in turmoil a distraught professor aggressively approached Mark and screamed, "Look at what you've done, look at what you've done!" Mark screamed back, "You've done it to yourself!" Minutes later he ran down the street, picked up a brick and smashed a Post Office window.[23] But this act of violence did not come naturally to him. It wasn't an emotional act as much as it was the result of ideology.

He had been moved to such dramatic behavior by the writings of his hero the late martyr to anti-imperialist revolution Che Guevara. Mark had come to the conclusion that the United States was the greatest imperialistic force in the world and that the American people should join hands with the people of the third world, particularly Vietnam, who were in a fierce struggle to resist US domination. He began to embrace the idea of the violent overthrow of the government of the United States and its capitalist system to be replaced, he envisioned, by a far more humane and socialistic society.

As time went on his advocacy for violence against the system flourished. He believed that antiwar activists were just not going far enough. Che had written, "Do it, don't just talk about it!" and Mark took that message very personally. He felt with all of his might that the war needed to be ended as quickly as possible and by any means necessary because millions of lives were at stake and US imperialism must be stopped once and for all. He embraced Che's theory of Foco (nucleus), which put forth the idea that future revolutionary armies would grow around the core of the guerilla band.

Mark, in June 1969, joined other members of the Weatherman faction on stage at the annual SDS convention and declared a break from SDS, thereby essentially causing the destruction of the most effective radical antiwar organization in the United States. The destruction of the organization was worth it to them because they believed that SDS was simply not militant enough and that they were ready to take the movement to new heights of violence and revolution.

Next, it was off to Chicago where a clarion call for thousands of young people to come and join in on the Days of Rage and take to the streets had been sounded. It was an effort to bring the war home and thereby let the people of the United States feel and see what was happening to people in war torn nations. They ended up with perhaps a few hundred demonstrators who raised Cain. Mark was left profoundly depressed by the trifling turnout and found himself at a turning point. The choice was to back-track to non-violent demonstrations or to go all in and ratchet up the violence. Driven by Che's ideology of international revolution against US imperialism Mark's decision was that they weren't radical enough and more violence was undoubtedly the answer.

Mark and the rest of the Weatherman organization wanted peace, justice and equality and thought that the movement of which they were a part would bring that about. They wanted to transform the whole system that gave America racism and the war. Of course that's really hard to do – if not impossible – but they had hopes. Mark and the others motivation was not one of criminality but rather "utopianism." They firmly believed that they could help to create the perfect society; one of justice, equality and peace.

When the townhouse in Greenwich Village exploded and instantly killed three of his Weatherman comrades Mark was already facing serious charges for his actions while inciting the Days of Rage and so he opted to join the Weather Underground Organization (WUO) and become a fugitive that was desperately wanted by the FBI.

The failure of the Days of Rage, the death of his three friends and the anxiety of fugitive life caught up with him as he became more and more depressed and even contemplated suicide. By the fall of 1970 he began to realize that he wasn't brave enough or committed enough to the revolution to go on. Harboring feelings of inadequacy he realized that he was not up for carrying out the revolutionary strategy the WUO called for, specifically the bombings, and he decided to separate himself from the group. By the dawn of 1971 he had severed his ties with the Weather Underground Organization.

Yet he remained underground for a defensive reason – the avoidance of prison. Over the next seven years he and his devoted wife and partner in the underground, Sue LeGrand, eluded the authorities by moving from place to place and State-to-State and adopted new identities wherever they went. The well-educated intellectual found himself toiling away at menial jobs in factories and on construction sites. He lived a precarious life wherein he was wanted by the police while struggling to just make ends meet economically. In the years before he had been an important and famous force in the antiwar movement and now he had become a nobody. He sat mournfully on the sidelines and watched while thousands of students in campuses all across America exploded in antiwar activism. He missed the movement that he helped to foment but now there was nothing that he could do but rue his miscalculations.

Finally, when the war came to its conclusion, Mark began to realize that the goal of overthrowing the government was nothing more than a fantasy. He had been wrong; not about opposing the war and imperialism but how he went about opposing it. Now he asked himself, "What's the point of continuing to hide? What's the point in running away?" The war was over and one by one members of the WUO began to surface and face the music. Mark concluded that he was prepared to do hard time in the penitentiary if necessary because anything would be better than living the life of an anonymous fugitive who could not even visit his beloved mother and father and introduce them to their grandson who was born in the underground.

He was lucky. Jimmy Carter had been elected President and wanted to make Vietnam a part of the past once and for all. Carter forgave the 35,000 young men who went to Canada to dodge the draft and his Democratic Justice Department had no heart for prosecuting former radicals. In addition, many charges against Mark had already been dropped because of the constitutional violations that the FBI committed under COINTELPRO. It turned out that he would not have to spend much time behind bars after all. His life as a radical revolutionary had come to an end at long last.[24]

TERENCE V. HAYES

Dozens of men in blue uniforms assembled on a Manhattan west side street corner near Columbia University, awaiting their orders. Among this army of police was Officer Terry Hayes (right). How strange the world had become for him. Terry could remember when Pearl Harbor was bombed and the United States entered

World War II. He wasn't even four years old yet and on the floor in the living room in his house in Brooklyn, his father was reading the funny papers to him when his mother came out of the kitchen with tears streaming down her face. The news blared out over the radio that America was at war.

During the next almost four years he learned how the United States could fight a war and win it. Everyone stood behind the cause for victory, everyone unquestioningly supported the service members. America took the gloves off, no holds barred, when fighting the Japanese and the Nazis. Films featuring people like the extremely popular movie star John Wayne demonstrated time and again how America would always win. Now Terry supported the cause in Vietnam and thought that America should win as it won World War II. He believed the US had an obligation to the people over there in Vietnam and that we should honor and protect our friends. However, those sentiments weren't shared by all of his comrades in blue. Although some volunteered and fought there were a number of the guys who said, "Hell no, I won't go!" and used their position as police officers to be exempted from the draft.

Terry, along with his partner Charlie Bennett (page 83), had been to plenty of demonstrations all around the city. He saw that there were always a couple of "rabble rousers in the crowd trying to whip up the rest of the group and then they'd melt back into the mass of people." Sometimes somebody might throw a rock and then the police would have to overpower him and haul him out. But the majority of the demonstrators, Terry noted, were just "pot smoking, longhaired hippie freaks" as the cops liked to call them. They were mellow, most of them, most of the time.

As Vietnam dragged on the demonstrations began to grow larger. Many were ad hoc affairs across from a recruiting station. They were quickly shut down. But the big ones were held at Foley Square, Times Square, and on College Campuses. After one demonstration Terry received a civilian complaint. "Pig! Pig!" They had come right up to him and shouted that in his face. He was ordered to hold the line but to let the demonstrators do, otherwise, whatever they wanted. Terry thought it would be funny to start making pig noises. "*Oink! Oink!*" Someone took his shield number and he had to go down to the Civilian Complaint Review Board. "You actually did that?" they asked in disbelief and he said, "Yeah, I did that." The chair of the board said, "Well, you know they have a right to protest. They could do anything but you can't say anything back." Terry just laughed and walked out. He got away with it.

There were lots of antiwar demonstrations all over the place and Terry was glad to participate in a counter-demonstration for once. It was a parade to "support the troops." A popular actor, named Chuck Connors, who was also a former baseball player and basketball star for the Brooklyn Dodgers and the Boston Celtics, was a big attraction as he marched near the front of the parade with lots of cops, including Officer Hayes, close by. Terry thought the parade to be well received. Anyhow, he didn't see anybody throw rocks at them.

Today was a different story as dozens of cops were assembled near Columbia. Demonstrators had taken over five of the University's buildings. The "usual suspects" started ramping up the crowds. Then Terry heard that the demonstrators threw a pair of huge flowerpots off the building and one of them, he was told, may have struck a policeman's horse and that's when the Inspector said, "I've had enough of this shit, let's get 'em! Go get 'em!" What looked to Terry to be about 500 cops went charging in and "wailed the shit" out of everybody and threw them all out. Dozens were injured and hundreds were arrested.

The mess he found inside of the building sickened him. "They were pissing in the corners and they were disgusting, filthy animals. I think they were in there at least three days." When the Inspector said, "Let's get 'em. Go get 'em," the cops were more than ready to go on the offensive. There was pent-up frustration by some of the guys who had been standing there for days and seething for years over the antiwar crowd. Terry was glad they "took care" of the demonstration. "You know what I mean, every time you had to go up there it was a pain in the ass. We used to tape the windows in the police cars so if somebody were throwing rocks they wouldn't break the windows."[25]

Judy Gumbo

Judy was what's known as a "red diaper baby" because her parents were communists. To be exact they were members of the Canadian Communist Party. As a result she grew up surrounded by progressive people, singing progressive songs and sharing their progressive ideas. In an effort to rebel against her authoritarian parents she moved to the United States where she soon met Yippie Stew Albert, whom she would marry. It wasn't long before she too became friends with Al-

bert's best friends, people like African-American activist Eldridge Cleaver and Yippie Jerry Rubin. Judy and Stew lived in New York and wanted to do everything they could to help stop the war. She saw Lyndon Johnson's "resignation" as a huge motivator to see if someone else could rise to power that was in the antiwar camp.

They began to help to plan demonstrations in Chicago at the soon to be held Democratic National Convention. When Robert Kennedy was assassinated Judy could sense an escalation in what she saw as fear caused by the "American culture of violence," yet Kennedy's death increased determination within the peace movement. When the summer and the convention came to Chicago Judy thought things didn't look promising to nominate a strong antiwar candidate and it appeared that it would be the establishment figure Hubert Humphrey.

When she arrived in the "Windy City" she strolled in Lincoln Park and thought, "How peaceful, how beautiful." She saw a few young people smoking grass, others hugging and kissing, while little old ladies walked white poodles in a slightly surreal bucolic scene. However, when night fell and darkness covered the park the place suddenly became eerie and weird. Judy looked over one of the hills and it appeared to her as if there was an invasion from outer space. There were bright lights with uniformed people marching in front of them and then teargas canisters flew through the air in an effort to get everyone out of the park – and so naturally she and the others ran. She ran as fast as she could but the gas was everywhere. She breathed in and started coughing violently while tears ran down her cheeks and although it was a very difficult experience it didn't make her feel at all fearful. Instead it made her feel empowered. She believed more than ever now that what she was doing, standing up against the establishment with the Yippies to end the war, was the right thing.

Her friend Eldridge Cleaver and the Black Panthers had originally used the term "Pig" as a descriptor for any oppressor that tried to thwart the will of the people. So Judy and the other Yippies thought that running a pig for President was a clear message that the people in charge of the government or were going to be elected and, therefore, were going to prosecute the war, were actually acting in a piggish way. The Yippies wanted to attempt to essentially expose the hypocrisy of the government and specifically the people who were running for President. Judy and a few other like-minded individuals went out and bought a live pig. She thought of it as more than just a stunt; it was a statement, albeit a funny one. A parade was held complete with "Secret Service Agents'" to protect their nominee: an animal that they christened Pigasus.

Later the beatings by the police started in earnest and Judy thought it wrong because the antiwar demonstrators were merely expressing themselves as any loyal American should and would do. While the police conducted their assaults Judy stood in the crowd and chanted along with everyone else, "The whole world is watching! The whole world is watching!" Indeed, the whole world was watching ... on television.

Months later when the Chicago 8 were brought to trial Judy attended. Her job was to send out the trial transcripts to all of the underground newspapers nationally and internationally. The distribution of this information heightened the drama of the case and gave people a really good sense of what was going on.

After the Chicago experience Judy and a small group of women went to North Vietnam to learn about the war first hand. She wanted to extend a hand of friendship in the name of peace and be able to return to the United States and speak with eyewitness knowledge about the state of the war.

As a result of her activism the FBI spied upon her and wrote in a confidential report;

> "The subject JUDY GUMBO is considered to be the most vicious, the most anti-American, the most anti-establishment, and the most dangerous to the internal security of the United States." [26]

SUSAN SCHNALL

Susan graduated from college having studied Science and Nursing and in one way she was among the lucky ones, because she didn't have to worry about student loans or scrounging up money however she could, like some of the other students that attended the prestigious Stanford University. She had a deal with the Navy in that they would pay for her tuition and she would return the favor by serving on active duty for three years from 1967 through 1969. Susan was always antiwar and she had even taken part in demonstrations before going into the service but she thought that she could assist in the healing of the many young soldiers that were wounded in Vietnam and help them to get on with their lives.

She was assigned to an old World War II-era hospital in Oakland, California which was made up of a series of barracks on stilts with each unit holding 35 or 40 wounded GI's and Marines. And so Susan witnessed first-hand and day after day over the next year the horrible effects of what she knew to be a senseless war. As time went on her antiwar feelings only intensified. Following the Tet Offensive she joined with others to organize a "GI and Veterans March for Peace" in San Francisco. She, working with the group, put fliers and posters up around the base advertising the upcoming demonstration but as quickly as she could post them they were torn down.

A frustrated Susan decided to take a page or two from the military's own playbook. She had watched General Westmoreland on television in full-dress uniform speaking to the press in favor of the war and asking for millions more dollars and tens of thousands more troops. She thought about how the military dropped leaflets while flying over Vietnamese villages to encourage them to enter into protective hamlets. She thought, "Hmm, television and airplanes. That's how we'll get the word out! If the United States could do that overseas then why couldn't we, as people for peace, drop fliers on military bases?"

Susan had a friend who was a pilot and she asked him to help her out. They took hundreds of their fliers and climbed aboard a rented single-engine plane and then up and away they went flying low over five military bases in the San Francisco Bay Area and "bombed" them with the announcement of the upcoming demonstration for peace. Next, for good measure, they flew over the deck of the USS *Ranger*, an aircraft carrier that was docked at Alameda Naval Air Station and "bombed" the ship. The newspaper and television reporters got wind of this daring action and wanted to know the details. Susan then held a press conference while proudly wearing her uniform just as she had seen Westmorland do. At the conference she said, "Yes, I did it. I'm a member of the military and against the war in South East Asia."[27]

A new regulation stipulated that military personnel could not wear a uniform while expressing political views, yet she had gone ahead and spoke at the rally anyway. Obviously, she was now in very deep trouble with the Navy and potentially faced a court martial and, if found guilty, as much as five years in a federal penitentiary at hard labor. The police estimated that 7,000 people attended the rally including some 200 active-duty GI's and perhaps another 100 Reservists and National Guardsmen along with at least a thousand veterans clad in partial uniform and christening themselves "Veterans for Peace." The numbers would have been higher but some members of the military were denied permission to leave the base that weekend because they were suspected of heading to the rally. This was the first time that a large number of active-duty members of the service voiced a public protest against the war. Those who dared to wear their uniforms believed that they could think of no greater cause to wear it than in the cause of peace.

Susan audaciously marched at the head of the five-block long parade beside a young Airman Michael Locks, who was also in uniform. She then stood in front of the large crowd and urged everyone to do what they could to "End the war now. Bring the boys home alive." She said that Vietnam "is a dirty, filthy war." Her speech was filmed and featured on the television news. Later the broadcast would be used as evidence at her court martial. Indeed, she was brought to trial and charged with a violation of Article 92 of the Uniform Code of Military Justice – conduct unbecoming an officer – for dropping the flyers on a military base "with intent to promote disloyalty, disaffection, and a weakening of morale among members of the armed services" and for wearing her uniform at the peace march.

The prosecuting attorney pushed for the maximum five years at hard labor. But at the conclusion she was found guilty and sentenced to six months.[28] [29] [30] Because regulations stipulated that a woman sentenced to less than a year would not necessarily go to prison, she served out her time in the pediatrics women's unit where she continued to organize against the war. Finally, Susan was dismissed from the service and upon her separation she moved to New York where she continued to work with GI's by forming coffee houses where they could go and discuss resistance to the war.

Her whole point was to bring attention to the issue of stopping the violence and say that members of the US military were against involvement in South East Asia. It was all very public and deliberate and it was all about bringing attention to another voice. Much later she would say, "I took care of the guys and tried to stop them from going to war. I loved my patients. It had been so painful to see what they had gone through and it was obvious to me that they were going to be suffering psychologically for years and years to come. I cared for the wounded from the war and tried to ease their pain and suffering. I used to ask the doctors about providing support for them. I remember they said, 'Oh, they'll get over it.' and I said, 'No, they won't!' I heard their screams in the middle of the night."[31] She learned that they wouldn't just "get over it." Post Traumatic Stress Disorder (PTSD) would haunt many for decades to come.

DEAN R. KAHLER

"**6**:30 son, time to get to work, it's 6:30." Dean's father would walk out the door in the morning on his way to his job at the Hercules Engine Company in Canton, Ohio. That was the signal for young Dean to head out too. He'd walk to his job a couple of times a week at the neighbor's farm about a hundred yards from his house and there he would milk cows for about an hour and a half. When finished he'd head home to wash, change his clothes, eat breakfast and catch the bus for school. After school he'd walk back to the farm and finish the job. When summer came Dean would work on the farm for a dollar a day, plus a gallon of milk and three meals. It was hard work but it was honest and it was the type of responsibility that built a young person's character.

The Kahler family were members of the "Church of the Brethren." This was considered by the government to be a peace church meaning its members did not believe in war because of strongly held religious convictions. In the early days of the United States' involvement in South East Asia when President Kennedy was sending advisors to Vietnam and most Americans never even heard of the place, members of the Kahlers' congregation, especially the women, were already organizing and protesting US involvement.

By the time Dean was 18 he did not believe in fighting in the war. He stood a good chance of being granted a deferment from carrying a weapon because he could be awarded Conscientious Objector (CO) status. First though he would have to jump through a lot of hoops. He had to write essays on why he objected to fighting in Vietnam, he was subjected to one-on-one interviews and later sat in front of a panel answering question after question about his personal religious beliefs. In the end he was granted the status but that would not prevent him from having to serve. He could still be inducted into the service and work in a non-combatant role.

When he reported to the induction center to take his physical he was told that he should wait one more day. That night a lottery was to be held live on national television. Many who were eligible for the draft and their loved ones watched with bated breath. 366 balls with a different date written on each one were placed in a glass jar. If the ball with your birth date was drawn early on then that meant it was likely that you would have to go into the military and possibly serve in Vietnam. On the other hand, If your birth date was chosen after 190 other dates … well then you'd count yourself among the lucky ones because you stood a great chance of not being drafted at all. Dean's number was 330! He was completely off the hook.

Nevertheless, he still had a strong desire to serve his country, just not in war. He decided that after he finished his education he would find some productive way to be of service to America. In March 1970 Dean arrived on the Ohio campus of Kent State University. He attended orientation, was assigned a room in the dorm and waited on the long lines to register for classes. It was more than a little exciting to be away from home for the first time and at the very beginning of what he hoped would be a wonderful learning experience.

One day, soon after his arrival, while he was taking a walk Dean noticed maybe twenty students pacing around, with signs, in a circle. The signs said things like "Stop the War" and "Peace Now." He also noticed, off to the side, four or five people wearing tennis shirts and holding rackets or golf clubs and they were shouting protests against the people who were protesting. After a while, as Dean listened to his new classmates more and more, he estimated that about one-third opposed the war, one-third supported the President and his efforts in Vietnam and one-third didn't care one way or the other.

Dean began to seriously evaluate the time that he lived in; "Young people are enjoying wonderful music, art, plays and literature but there's also riots, terror and anxiety. The Draft looms over many people's heads like a Damocles sword. One wrong move and you could be dressed in an olive drab uniform, sent off to basic training and become part of the cannon fodder being sent to South East Asia."[32]

Meanwhile, on Thursday April 30th, President Nixon announced that some American troops had left Vietnam and gone into Cambodia to bring the fight to the Vietnamese that were amassed there. This announcement outraged a number of the Kent State students and the following night confrontations with the police in town led to violence and destruction.[33] On Saturday night someone set fire to the Reserve Officers Training Corps (ROTC) building where some students went for preparation before entering the military.[34] And so it was that on the pleasant spring morning of Monday May 4th, 1970, Dean awoke and could immediately sense the tension in the air. The night before the Governor had assigned the National Guard to go to Kent State and "protect" the students and the property from further harm.

When Dean climbed out of his bed and peered out the window he was shaken by the sight of Armored Personnel Carriers and two-and-half ton Army trucks rumbling down the streets of the campus. Worried, he met with a few of the other students on his floor and they agreed to go up to the Commons area to see what was going on. They had heard that there was going to be some sort of a gathering or rally to discuss recent events. Having grown up spending much of his time on the farm and with school activities he did not have the opportunity to participate in any of the Civil Rights protests or antiwar demonstrations and so he didn't know what to expect.

Before leaving he called his Professor and said that he was going to miss class that morning but would see him later in the lab. The Professor sounded concerned, "Be careful and take care of yourself." Naively Dean thought his teacher was being a bit more dramatic than was necessary. After all, this was the very heartland of America. He was safe. What harm could possibly come to him? The Commons was a central gathering place for the students. It was about the size of three or four football fields. It was a big, pleasant and inviting grassy area. This was the first warm day at Kent that year and so there were many students wandering about or casually sitting on the grass talking about this and that. Some were eating snacks, others were reading and still others were participating in "teach-ins" about the war.

When Dean and his friends first arrived they were greeted by the squawk of a student making a speech through a bullhorn. Some students were standing around and listening. The speaker was carrying on about all the "isms" of the day. Communism, capitalism, sexism, racism, you name it. Dean paused to think, "What the heck does this have to do with the expansion of the war into another country?" He glanced across the commons and there witnessed a chilling sight; dozens of soldiers in combat gear and armed with rifles. Soon some Guardsmen were circling around them in a jeep and ordering everyone to disperse. They announced that the gathering of more than four people at a time was in violation of some emergency code or emergency law. The problem was, no one thought that there was an emergency inasmuch as they were all just doing what they normally did.

A few students began to grow indignant and threw rocks towards the jeep and one of them actually bounced off the vehicle's hood. Many students began to boo and jeer. Some cursed or held up their middle finger in a gesture of derision, defiance and disdsain. Insults began to fly freely, "Pigs off campus!!!" and "We don't want your stinking war!!!" The jeep withdrew. About five minutes later Dean saw the same jeep as it rumbled to the center of the Commons. The soldiers again announced that the students had gathered illegally. They read something called "The Riot Act" and said they would force them to disperse. Dean was perplexed. There was no "riot" going on. He saw only a peaceful gathering of students on a warm, sunny day in May. Many students booed, jeered and chanted slogans while the jeep turned around and retreated to their lines.

Dean glanced at his watch. It was about 12:15 and he considered heading back and getting ready for his 1:10 class. Then he thought he'd stay for a few more minutes, "Okay, I'll see what happens here." Then the troops began to form into lines, putting on gas masks, fixing bayonets and checking their weapons for what looked to Dean like ammunition. Unlike many other students that day Dean assumed that the guns were loaded. He had National Rifle Association (NRA) hunting training and believed that the only gun that you should assume to be empty was the one you've checked yourself. All of a sudden the soldiers began to launch tear gas grenades. This created quite a stir as students began to move about and go up a little hill and around the back of one of the buildings. Dean and a few others stayed behind. A couple of students daringly lobbed tear gas canisters back in the direction of the Guardsmen.

By the time the students came out from behind the building Dean had gotten a dose of the tear gas, as did most of the others. There was construction going on and there was a pile of gravel. A good place to take cover as he wiped at his eyes with wet napkins. He dropped down behind it as he watched the soldiers, bayonets bristling in the sunshine, shoulder-to-shoulder march across the field and up the hill. A few soldiers pointed their weapons at students. Dean thought, "Oh man, what the heck are these people doing? You don't threaten somebody by pointing a weapon at them – that's the stupidest thing you could do."

When the soldiers got to the bottom of the hill in the practice football field some of them formed a huddle as a team would during a game. Dean saw them looking over their shoulders at students, mostly those closest to them. Then the troops formed up again and marched back across the field. Dean didn't see anyone throw anything at the soldiers or attacking them. Clearly the soldiers were not in any serious physical danger, he concluded. Hundreds of students stood off to the side watching the action as if at a sporting event or some sort of weird pageant. Others stayed on the Hill while they continued to taunt the soldiers. As the men marched away Dean felt safe. The soldiers were blocked in on three sides by a fence and in front were students forming a fourth fence. The students parted before them like the Red Sea as the guardsmen marched on.

They were about a hundred yards away when suddenly a group of soldiers wheeled around and brought their weapons to their shoulders. Dean thought, "Oh my God, they're going to shoot!" It didn't add up. People who were there to protect life and property were now about to literally murder the students. At that exact moment they opened fire and continued to fire for thirteen seemingly endless seconds. At six feet three inches with bright red hair Dean made an obvious target. With no place to hide he hit the dirt, getting down as low as he possibly could. He heard bullets hitting the ground all around him. People began to fall. Four were killed right away while nine others were wounded. Dean felt something like the sting of a bee. A bullet hit him in the back. He knew immediately that he had experienced a spinal cord injury. A few students stopped to try and help him. A new friend and member of the Black Student Union, Robert Picket, ran up to him and asked Dean for his parents' phone number and then ran off to call them and report that Dean had been wounded but was alive. He was not bleeding externally but he knew he was bleeding internally because he could feel the pressure building in his chest and he knew it was blood filling up in his abdominal and chest cavity.

Minutes ticked away as he waited for an ambulance. It felt like an hour had passed but it was closer to fifteen minutes before it arrived. The National Guard unit had ambulances but no one thought to send them to help the wounded students and they didn't even bother to radio for help or report that they had just shot over a dozen unarmed college students in cold blood.

At the hospital Dean lay on a gurney in the hallway listening to the frantic interaction of doctors, nurses and wounded. Then to his surprise a Minister friend of the family was standing by his side. He happened to be in the hospital and Dean's mother called and asked him to look out for her wounded son. The Minister and Dean prayed and soon his clothes were cut off and he was wheeled into the operating room. It was Monday afternoon. When he next opened his eyes it was Friday. First came the pain followed by the terrifying noises of all the machines clicking, clacking, sucking, blowing and hissing as they pumped fluids into him and took fluids out. Another device pumped air into him and took air out.[35]

Throughout his recovery he received support from family, friends and his church. On the other hand, hateful and ignorant people often directed their rage at him. For example, he opened a letter that began, "Dear Communist Hippie Radical, I hope by the time you read this, you are dead." In addition, a poll showed that 58% of Americans thought that the students were responsible for the aggression. Richard Nixon blamed the students saying, "When dissent turns to violence, it invites tragedy."[36] Slowly, as time went by, Dean began to recover but he would never walk again.[37]

DENNY MEYER

Denny Meyer's mother, who was an illegal immigrant, taught him when he was still a toddler that there is nothing more precious than American freedom. Both of his parents were World War II holocaust refugees from Nazi Germany. When he was in his late teens Vietnam was in full swing but he didn't have to concern himself with being drafted because he had a double deferment. One, he was enrolled in college and two, he was gay.

Denny witnessed with his own eyes some antiwar protesters as they burned the American flag. His flag! The thought of the flag burning angered him and he felt a strong need to do something. He thought, "It's time to pay my country back for my famiy's freedom." And so he would go out and join up. He thought about which branch of the service he wanted, "Well, I like the sea and I like the bell-bottomed Navy uniforms. Also," he surmised, "in the Navy I'd always have a bed to sleep in as opposed to sleeping in a muddy foxhole." And so it was that Denny joined the Navy.

He told his gay friends about what he did and they said, "You're crazy. You can't do that. You're a little faggot." And he responded, "Watch me." Next Denny went home and told his parents what he had done and they said "Seite meshuga?" which translates as, "Are you crazy?" They said, "You're supposed to be a doctor or a lawyer." Soon his induction day arrived and there were countless people at the center. A very busy place that operated as would a factory production line. He went from one station to the next; the eye doctor told him to read the chart on the wall, then the next doctor listened to his heart, then someone peered into his ears and so on and so on.

Finally, Denny stepped up in front of the psychologist. He had been dreading this all day because he had been waiting for "the" question. At this time thousands of young Americans were heading off to Canada to avoid the draft. Thousands of other young straight Americans were lying and saying they were gay also to avoid the draft. Ironically, Denny wanted to say that he was straight so that he could serve, yet he was not comfortable about lying. And so it was that with no small amount of trepidation he stepped in front of the psychologist who was busy rubber-stamping papers and never even looked up. The doctor just muttered, "Any problem with homosexuality?" That was the question and of course being a wise guy he thought to himself, "Well, I don't have any problem with being a homosexual." He felt he could honestly answer, "No." And without missing a beat the doctor stamped his papers, barked, "Next!" and that was that. As soon as he walked on to the next station he thought to himself, "Well, now you've done it." Then he was sworn in.

After boot camp Denny was assigned to the aircraft carrier USS *Forrestal*. The year before, while in the Gulf of Tonkin off the coast of North Vietnam, a catastrophic fire killed 134 sailors and injured 161 others. The ship was under massive industrial repair in Norfolk, Va. when Denny was one of nearly 400 replacements sent to the ship and had to walk through clouds of toxic dust while the Forrestal was under repair for six months. (This exposure resulted in his developing near-fatal cancer many decades later.) Once on the ship he was assigned to a sleeping compartment. Somebody bellowed, "Find a bunk." He saw an empty top bunk and claimed it. The other sailors gave him a funny look. Later he discovered that the previous occupant had been burned to death on that very spot during the big fire.

When he reported for his duty assignment the Petty Officer noticed that Denny had some clerical know-how. (When he was twelve his mother had sent him to summer school to learn typing.) He was assigned to type reports and assist the officers. Naturally his mother was grateful that he became a clerk instead of a warrior. His performance was deemed to be outstanding and so he was promoted every year. Eventually he was reassigned to Headquarters in Norfolk, Virginia where he worked in a unit called "Secret Files." The Chief that ran the office was a kindly middle-aged straight man with a wife and three children but he figured out what he had with Denny. He had a gay sailor. He knew that Denny had the talent to do his job well and the Chief played the role of what Denny thought of as a "mother hen." If things began to sound a bit campy the Chief would arch an eyebrow as if to say, "Watch it." "It" could never be openly acknowledged, "it" could never be said.

At one point Denny was required to get a top-secret clearance for his work. So one day he was ordered to meet with two CID agents who informed him that they were conducting a routine investigation for his clearance and so they asked questions and finally one of them said, "We have found that you are a …" and between that word and the next Denny died a thousand deaths. He thought, "Oh God, they found out! Now I'm going to be kicked out in disgrace." He imagined three months of intense interrogation followed by a dishonorable discharge. Then the agent finished the sentence and he said, "user of marijuana." At which point Denny wanted to laugh and clap his hands and jump up and shout, "Oh, is that all?" But he knew better and so he just looked perplexed. It turned out that they routinely said that to everyone to watch for their reaction.

He had been so distressed, thinking that he had been "outed," that he just wanted to get away from there and run to the Men's room and vomit. But he got his clearance and went back to the office sweating and looking green around the gills. The Chief stared at him and said, "What happened?" Denny didn't say anything but the Chief figured out what had rattled him and he just looked at him with a twinkle in his eyes as if to say, "I get it." But again, "it" could never, ever be discussed.

Periodically investigators would conduct a witch-hunt in a search for gay people. Denny got so good at hiding his true self that he developed a reputation of being the straightest guy around. One day the officers were on a witch-hunt looking for men they called "queers" and they ordered him in. They said, "Meyer, you're the only one we can be sure of who's straight." He didn't know whether to laugh or cry as he thought, "I'm the one they're looking for. Are these guys dumb or crazy?" They said, "Will you help us find these people so we can get rid of them?" He knew exactly what to do. He played the role of a dumb sailor and said, "I dunno nothin bout dat, sir." In exasperation they said, "Get out of here Meyer." Which is exactly what he wanted them to say.

Denny knew that if other service members even thought that you were gay, in those days, you could be murdered. In Vietnam you might be fragged, that is shot in the back or killed by a fragmentation grenade. In the Navy you might be thrown overboard. Or if you survived you'd be intensely interrogated for three months and then less than honorably discharged. And the interrogations focused on learning the names of everybody you knew so that they could haul them in and interrogate them. That's what it was all about.

That's how the witch-hunt worked. They would drag you in and tell you they know you're gay and they'd scare you to death and tell you that you'd go to jail for the rest of your life. So they'd get you to talk and then they'd haul in all those you named and get them to talk and that's how it grew and grew. It always rose through the ranks and invariably they'd call upon a low-level sailor to terrorize until he'd name a few higher up than himself and so on and eventually it'd get to a pretty high-ranking officer. Whenever these interrogators became overly zealous and kept going higher and higher eventually they'd get a call from the Pentagon saying, "Stop!" They were getting too close to some of the top men.

Denny kept his big secret yet it was incredibly hard to serve in silence and be gay. It seemed that almost every single day he'd hear death threats. Other sailors would describe in frightening detail what they would do if they ever found "one" and of course he was an invisible minority. No one knew that the guy who was standing right next to them as they talked about killing queers was himself gay. He listened to crude and violent jokes and had to laugh along with everybody or else they'd look at him and say, "What's your problem?"

Later Denny served in the Army Reserve in San Francisco. He had risen rapidly through the ranks but the higher an enlisted man went the closer he was observed. He was becoming more and more nervous that they would find out his true nature. He was worried that somebody would see him at the supermarket with his partner, for instance. Denny was always looking over his shoulder waiting to be caught. He, along with many thousands of others served in silence and again he heard bigoted comments every single day from people he thought were his friends. In the end when it was time to "re-up" once more he decided that he had enough and left.[38]

JIM CONNELLY

Jim was a creative kid and a dreamer. He was going through some changes, psychologically. He had been suspended from school for poor academic performance but it was like he almost didn't care, almost as if he wanted to be drafted. And sure enough before he knew it he was going through training and then on his way to his duty assignment as an artillery surveyor in Cu Chi, Vietnam.

During his time there he wasn't shot at very often and, therefore, didn't have to shoot at a lot of people himself. Which is the way he wanted it. Half of his time was spent back at headquarters and was just plain boring, filled with prosaic tasks like burning human excrement or he was out in the field in a jeep, surveying gun batteries with the rest of the crew.

He knew of people who were smuggling sapphires and there was a lot of drug activity, it was kind of a lawless experience, kind of anarchic – it was a bizarre type of world. When Jim was in Vietnam he saw places that were untouched by the city culture, places way out in the countryside that were just plain beautiful, charming little hamlets. The cities held their charms too. Saigon, for instance, was nicknamed the Paris of the Orient.

After his relatively uneventful tour of Vietnam he returned to Upstate New York to live in his parents' home, play in rock bands and get a job with General Electric. He took a few classes at the local college on the GI Bill but found it just wasn't for him. Then one day Jim happened to hear about a concert that was coming to the region – something called "Woodstock." Among Jim's favorite groups was one that not a lot of people knew about, The Incredible String Band, from England. He heard they were going to play and he thought, "Well that's interesting."

He took a loaf of bread and a jar of peanut butter and put it in a sack, climbed into his Mustang, drove off and tried to get to the concert. The roads were all blocked and so he would go down one road until it started to get too congested, turn around and head off and take another. He kept going right, turning right, kept going in as far as he could, determined to get there. He finally worked his way around until he found a road that seemed pretty close to the concert venue. He parked the car and started walking with hundreds of other young people. It was just great to be walking along with all these other folks who were all talking about what the great music was going to be like and not have to worry that somebody might be hiding in the woods trying to kill him.

He fell in with this one bunch who were all Credence Clearwater fans and were all talking about, "Oh, its gonna be great 'cause everybodies gonna be 'chooglin'." He had no idea what "chooglin" meant. "What the devil is that?" He guessed, correctly, that it's a term from one of Clearwater's songs. When he finally got to the place he simply walked in. It was a "free" concert. He had a piece of plastic to keep the rain off of him and something to sit on but precious little water to drink.

Jim wandered past the place where "The Diggers" had tents set up and they were providing talk-downs for people who had taken the wrong kind of LSD and also a little water and food and a kind of rough medical facility to help people. He walked down in front, which was a very muddy area, right in front of the stage where all the water collected. In addition, there was a pretty high wall in front of the stage so you couldn't really see anything, but people kind of just made that trip and so there was a river of people going through there and all coming back out again on the other side.

Jim was able to get through all three days all right. He really didn't expect luxury accommodations and was happy to find dry pieces of grass to sit on. If he stayed up on the top of the hill it was not too bad. He heard warnings from the stage against taking the bad brown acid (LSD). He witnessed Abbie Hoffman getting up on stage and grabbing the microphone and Peter Townshend of The Who whacking him with the end of his guitar. Jim felt sorry for Abbie because he agreed with his message stating that a man named John Sinclair was in prison for ten years for possessing two marijuana cigarettes and that he should be set free. Anyway, that's what Jim thought that he was trying to talk about.

He did get to see The Incredible String Band but they had technical problems and their sound didn't come out well. They were having trouble getting over the PA system but one thing that he would never forget that they did was a pagan invocation to the four directions, which to Jim launched the spiritual value of the whole scene. Santana played during the beginning and they were pretty amazing. He saw Canned Heat and they impressed him. He never thought too much of them before but when he saw them live he thought, "Wow, pretty intense."

He saw Crosby, Stills and Nash doing Sweet Judy Blue Eyes. Just to see these three guys come out live and do this complicated arrangement was something that blew peoples' minds. Country Joe and the Fish led everybody in the Fish Cheer, "One, two, three. What are we fighting for?" He saw Richie Havens right at the beginning of the concert. At night Sly and the Family Stone were playing "Want to take you Higher" and everybody was just going nuts. Jefferson Airplane had taken the stage and he had been sleeping and waking up, sleeping and waking up and they were playing right at sunrise. They had the Joshua Light Show going on behind them. They were one of the pioneers, projecting various blobs and psychedelic images behind them on a screen. The sunrise was drowning out the Joshua light show, but what a beautiful sunrise with the Jefferson Airplane playing! So that was a good moment too. He heard Janis Joplin sing and Jimi Hendrix perform the Star Spangled Banner.

He stayed for the whole thing and survived on peanut butter and what other people, strangers, shared with him. It was continuous music nearly all day and night for three days and nights. The organizers didn't really have their stage craft down well enough to get bands on and off and they didn't really have a firm schedule as to who would play in what order so they just kept putting people on whenever they could get them on. The schedule was incompetent and there were periods where there was no music and he would fall asleep and then wake up and there would be some amazing band playing.

When it was all over he hung around for a while. He wanted to see what the aftermath was. There was just all this stuff that people left in the mud and that disappointed him because he expected that people would clean up after themselves. He had the notion that the hippie nation would be more conscious of the environment. There were some people with big garbage sacks picking stuff up but mostly it was just sort of a destroyed field.

Following the concert he returned to his hometown exhausted but glad. His friends knew that he had been in the service but no one ever really talked about it. It just was not a big topic. The people Jim hung with were more the hippie type of person, the counter-culture. He thought they felt sorry for him and for people who went to Vietnam and they were sympathetic. It wasn't a topic brought up by a lot people. One friend who knew about Jim's service said, "You're a veteran why don't you go apply for a civil service job?" Jim took a test and wound up working at the VA as a medical technician.[39]

E.J. DIONNE, JR.

E.J. grew up in a household that was pretty political. His dad was a conservative and E.J. was a liberal. They argued politics all the time, but it was never nasty because they both enjoyed debating. Ironically it was his father that first spoke out against the fighting in Vietnam. Although E.J., Sr. had served in the Army during World War II he had no bad personal experiences with war but he just thought that, in general, it was a terrible idea. E.J. then, too, developed anti-Vietnam War sentiments.

In the summer of 1968 he and his dad went to visit an old Army buddy in a cottage on Long Island Sound in Connecticut. Together, they huddled around the television set and watched the Democratic National Convention. When the Party put forth a peace plank the two found themselves not debating but, for the first time that he could remember, rooting for the same side. They were on the side for peace. Sadly, not long after that E.J.'s dad passed away.

Following his father's loss he was living with an Uncle for a while and E.J. and his cousin used the basement as a kind of a hang-out. One night E.J. went down, pen in hand, and worked really hard on a statement to his draft board. Write and read, rewrite and reread time and time again. Tired, he laid his work down and instead began to write a letter of support for his friend, who was in the same boat as he. That was easy because he had no doubt about what he was writing. Then he went back to his own statement and resumed the struggle. He knew, perhaps with a touch of vanity, that he was a very good writer and that technically there was nothing wrong with what he had written. Yet there was something about this statement. Something that just would not ring true.

"Am I, in all honesty, a Conscientious Objector?" he wondered. There was no question that his father's thoughts and Daniel Berrigan's writings and acts of civil disobedience had a strong influence on the Catholic teenager and so when he reported for draft registration he had checked off a box on the official form and thereby applied for CO status. However, in the end E.J. knew that he was actually a believer in a "just" war. He thought one could not be selectively conscientiously objecting – you either opposed all war or you did not. If it were Nazis, for example, or if some enemy invaded the United States, he thought, "Sure, I'd go in the Army."

He knew that the war in Vietnam was all wrong. He had studied the situation carefully, discussed it, prayed about it, wrestled with it. But the truth, he believed, was that he did not qualify for CO status. Instead of submitting his completed application he wrote to his draft board and withdrew his request, thus making himself eligible to be inducted. Soon thereafter he was spared having to serve because he received a relatively high lottery number. Nonetheless, he felt that he needed to do something for the others who had to go. He wanted to help to end the war.

A man in his hometown who had become a father figure to him was a businessman and a founder of the Vietnam Moratorium, an effort to organize a national day of a call for peace. And so E.J. became active in moratorium politics. They organized. He liked the original approach to the moratorium, which was a march in peoples' own communities throughout the United States. Through their efforts the working-class town of Fall River, Massachusetts turned out about 3,000 people to march on the moratorium day. Then he also helped to organize when President Nixon ordered the invasion of Cambodia. At this point he was a student at Harvard and he and a friend made it possible for busloads of students to go down to Washington. They lobbied Congress to cut funding for the Vietnam invasion.

That became a very important piece of his life, inspiring him, ultimately, to work on Democrat George McGovern's Presidential campaign in 1972 against Richard Nixon. This, of course, was when Nixon's "plumbers" burglarized the Watergate headquarters of the Democratic National Committee. E.J. saw the irony because Nixon was going to beat McGovern anyway, without committing any illegal acts. He knew they were going to lose that election and that, to him, was one of the craziest things about Watergate.

He was always very anti-violence at demonstrations. He thought it was just plain wrong and counter-productive and he felt strongly that burning the American flag was a disgraceful act. One of his favorite quotations of that period was from Norman Thomas – a great American Socialist who said, "If you want a symbolic gesture, don't burn the flag; wash it." E.J. would add the words, "with reverence."

He thought many times that had that been the approach, the message sent would have been radically different. Obviously he had sympathy for the goals of the antiwar protesters and thought they shouldn't be treated the way they were by the police, but he really did believe that they could be, at times, their own worst enemy. E.J. and his companions wanted people to understand that they weren't against the war because they hated their country; they were against the war because they loved their country. They thought America was making a mistake.

They were trying to persuade people who held a strong sense of old-fashioned patriotism to oppose the war and E.J. felt that they weren't reaching that segment of society. It seemed as though at times they were talking to themselves; preaching to the choir as it were. Sometimes, he thought, it was about people expressing their own righteousness rather than actually persuading people that the war was a mistake. That's what led him to electoral politics, like Paul Booth did, because he thought you were trying, actually trying, to win an election and persuade people to use their democratic rights to end the war and make the other important changes that America so desperately needed to make.[40]

KATHLEEN GUNSON

She was raised in rural Oregon surrounded by beautiful bucolic fields and orchards and cows and she lived an idyllic childhood in this quaint setting. However, even by the time Kathleen was seven she just knew she wanted to see the world and all of the amazing things that it had to offer her. As a child Kathleen loved reading a series of books about a young woman, Cherry

Ames, who enjoyed exciting adventures. The series included *Cherry Ames, Army Nurse* and *Cherry Ames, Flight Nurse* and *Cherry Ames, Veteran's Nurse*. She also loved old World War II movies that featured nurses and so it was quite natural that by the time she was out of high school she was itching to go to nursing school and then to join the Army.

She, thinking it a romantic and an exciting challenge, volunteered to go to Vietnam. Kathleen was commissioned an officer and sent to Phu Bai's (foo–by) 85th Evacuation Hospital. There, within the protective bubble of the hospital, she didn't know where the casualties were coming from and why the enemy was so close. Wanting to get out and see a bit more of the country, she asked the Colonel if she could go to Danang and have a look around. "Permission denied. Too dangerous." The Colonel growled. She thought, "Well, I'm gonna go anyway." With a fully loaded .45 that she purchased on the black market she hopped into a jeep when a soldier walked up and handed her an M-16. So she drove out and saw a bit of "Nam" and in the end she was fine. One evening, soon thereafter, in the Officer's Club she went over to the Colonel and said, "Okay, you can punish me now because I went against your orders. Because I wanted to have an adventure." The Colonel responded, "Well, I know you went." And she said, "Well, how do you know that?" And he said, "Well, how do you think you got that M-16 issued to you today." Then he said, "Will you not do things like that again? I don't want to have to write your parents and tell them that you were killed."

By then the war was winding down and the 85th became the most northern hospital. The influx of patients would vary. They got them but it wasn't like the '68-'69 casualty load because by '70-'71 most soldiers realized that the war was unwinnable. Kathleen thought that they were being used as cannon fodder. And so a "frag" might occur when some young ROTC academy officer would say, "We're going to go out and do a search and destroy." They'd go out and there would be these needless deaths. Some of the guys would finally get fed up and say, "Enough." They would rig, perhaps, a hand grenade under the cot of the Sergeant, Lieutenant or Captain, whoever ordered the senseless mission, or they would toss a grenade in on him or he would be "accidentally" shot from behind. The grenade victims would be brought in leaking blood from hundreds of penetrating little wounds. Often these men could not be saved. Also, Kathleen discovered that there was mutiny occurring but the officers didn't want to call it mutiny, so they called it something like "refusal to engage." She also treated a lot of heroin overdoses, saw accidents with guys with their handguns and cared for a good number of soldiers after their suicide attempts.

And then one day they would accept seven or eight casualties in Company A, for instance, and the next thing she'd get Company B and a soldier would report, "We went to retrieve the dead from Company A. They had seven dead out there and now we have an additional nine casualties." And the next thing you know here comes Company C and they had been sent to extract Company B's dead and wounded and they took casualties too. It was in Kathleen's view a senseless, useless nightmare. She tried to find ways to be happy and so she partied a lot, played baseball and watched movies. So it wasn't always gloomy and it kept her from going mad.

Once one of the surgical wards received a squad of GI's. These guys had been out in the bush and had wounds, nothing life threatening; they were going to be sent back out as soon as the hospital could discharge them. They might have been shot through the arm or shot through the leg in a fleshy part. Most had infections that she and the other hospital staff had to put drains into and that kind of thing. The soldiers had been out there for maybe seven, eight, nine days and they tended not to do a lot of hygiene if they could help it. They were filthy and had hair in need of trimming, were in desperate need of shaves, had dirty fingernails and lice. Some officer came in and gave them grief for their appearance and so she looked at her corpsmen and she said, "We'll go around and ask people if they want their heads washed and their hair cut and we'll do fingernails and toenails." So she set up a real "beauty parlor."

She became the shampooer. A corpsman clipped the fingernails. Not wanting to worry about cutting anybody's throat, she had another corpsman do the shaving and another one, who had been a barber in the States, did all the haircuts. They had them shipshape in a couple of hours and it was fun because it was something different and for a few hours everyone had a good time and forgot about the senseless war.[41]

Jim Schmidt

Phu Bai was a little village in between the provincial capital of Hue and the bustling city of Danang. Jim Schmidt and his comrades in the Second Brigade were stationed there on a firebase called "Brick." Just a few short months earlier he was at home messing around fixing cars and going to college. But things changed later on in 1970 when college students were no longer exempt from the draft. And so it was that after his sophomore year Jim was called upon to serve. Base security was the main part of his job and so he and his unit regularly ran patrols in small groups called squads. They'd march out into the surrounding jungle in the daytime ("Charlie owned the night.") and search for enemy soldiers in an effort to prevent them from setting up artillery or mortars within range of the firebase. The war had changed by this time – it was no longer about body counts. It was about hanging on until the South Vietnamese could take the responsibility for defending themselves and America could get the hell out of there at last.

Jim definitely did not want to go to Vietnam. The war had already been a part of his life for a long time and he knew how ugly things could get. In 1965, when the Marines charged ashore in Danang and the US began to take over the war, he was 15. By the time he was drafted five years later it seemed like he almost couldn't remember a time when we weren't at war. He had had friends go and come back and their discussions, when they would talk about it, were not pleasant and by that point it was very obvious that there wasn't going to be a military solution to what he saw as just a mess. He believed that whatever solution we would eventually have would be a political one and so it began to look more and more foolish to throw soldiers into a meat grinder when you could not see a military end. They were not fighting to gain some sort of advantage or conquer some amount of territory or villages; they were there to stay alive and honestly, he thought, so were the North Vietnamese and the Viet Cong.

When they made contact with the enemy Jim thought neither side had much stomach for the fight. No one wanted to be, as Jim saw it, the last person to die for this massive stupidity. By about 1970 the Army in Vietnam was pretty dysfunctional. It had discipline problems, it had drug problems, it had you-name-it problems. Jim was certain that even Nixon knew it. It was not a stellar time for the US military and he laid that right at the feet of the politicians and the way they handled this war from the onset.

He and the soldiers with whom he served took their orders and figured out ways to do most of what was wanted of them, but to do it as safely as possible. So if they were given an order to go from Point A to Point B and walk along a certain road that they did not think was safe they would simply refuse. They would find a way to get to Point B that didn't involve walking along that road and by that time the officers and senior Non Commissioned Officers (NCO's) had figured out that was the way it was going to be.

Jim knew that questioning orders and making them work to your advantage is definitely a sign of a dysfunctional military operation. In certain situations rank became almost meaningless because what gave someone the authority to lead or to be listened to was "time in country." If someone said, "Ok, I'm a First Lieutenant and I've been in country three weeks." Jim knew he had almost no chance of anybody giving him any credibility at all. On the other hand a Private First Class (PFC) who survived ten months in country has obviously figured something out and "you're gonna listen to this guy." So Jim realized that in the end you're turning the military protocol upside down and by definition that's a dysfunctional army. He couldn't speak to how widespread this was because he was never in another area but he suspected that was a general attitude.

His movement and contact with the civilian population was limited and so there was never even the remotest possibility of a situation like My Lai (me-lie) where hundreds of civilians were murdered by American soldiers. They were dropped in Point A and they were going to be picked up at Point B and their job was to sanitize the area in between and that was pretty much it.

When they had contact with the enemy it was a single individual or a very small group of three or four. He was never in any major battalion-size battles. When he returned fire at the enemy he felt like he was shooting at ghosts. The jungle's vegetation was so thick that typically all he'd maybe see was a muzzle flash, maybe not.

They knew what to do when they engaged the enemy. They'd call in the cobras, the attack helicopters, and the Vietcong knew that too and they realized that they had a certain amount of time until the cobras got there and that's how long it lasted. A couple of minutes, two or three minutes maybe, which is a long time at which to be shot. It was repeated enough that they knew what the VC were going to do and the VC knew what the Americans were going to do. Each side kind of played their roles out in that way.

Month after month they explored the jungle meeting with equally small patrols of VC, engaging them in a firefight for a few minutes until the enemy ran off as air-support loaded with ordnance raced to the scene.

The Americans were dependent upon one another and their goal was quite simple, for each one to stay alive. Morale didn't change because of any external stuff like antiwar demonstrations at home. Plus, there was nothing any General could come up and tell them to give any kind of joy at all, even though they tried. Their morale was good when they were all alive and it suffered when one of them got hurt or killed, period.

Jim would not take Rest and Recuperation (R and R). He would not enjoy a week in Tokyo or in Sydney to unwind and recharge the batteries as the rest of his squad had done. Yes, he could see himself, in his mind's eye, not in worn jungle fatigues but wearing comfortable civilian clothes while he casually strolled down a busy yet peaceful avenue in Australia. No one would be trying to kill him there and he would not be trying to kill anyone else.

Jim knew that the stress would lift off of his shoulders as he walked along and it would simply float high, high and away into the stratosphere. He would be free of war and of Vietnam. He could see himself turn a corner and decide that he would not go back at all. Yes, he could pretty much guarantee that he would not go back to that rotten stinking jungle. And so for that reason he would not take R and R.

His last month was a little different. He must have begun to exhibit scary signs because one of the Staff Sergeants in charge pulled him aside one day and said, "Stay here for a second, Smitty." Everyone else was up to where the helicopters were and he said, "I'm gonna keep you here a couple of days and see how you're doing."

He hadn't asked for any special treatment and he actually thought he was doing okay, but it had been eleven months. He figured he must have been pretty burnt out and it was showing. He ended up being on security in Phu Bai when the famous comedian Bob Hope came to do a show that Christmas. So that was pretty cool. Soon thereafter he went back to the United States.

At the time that he returned Jim had no idea about French Colonialism or any of the things that went on in Vietnam's history before his being there. He had no idea what the Vietnamese people had put up with. When he learned the history, he thought, that's kind of what our country is about; we're unwilling to be somebody else's colony or to have someone else govern us and tell us what our laws should be. Jim came to believe that their situation in the occupation of Vietnam was very similar to our own situation during the Revolutionary War. We would never surrender back then. That was not an option. Neither could they surrender.

Had the politicians taken the time to figure that out before we went in there it would have made all the difference in the world, he thought. There's almost no way to compare how our history would have been different had we understood that early on. People like Robert McNamara should have understood it but foolishly and arrogantly kept shoveling men and material and money into what Jim thought was this nutty cause. Jim found it interesting to learn more about it but it was also very frustrating to learn how the war was bungled at all levels. In some ways he felt he would have been better off if he didn't know.

He was discharged in February '72 and returned to California. It was tough to put into words what it was like. The best way to put it is he thought the whole world had changed and gone crazy and it turned out he was the one who had changed. He had been looking at things through an old set of prisms and now he was looking at things in a new way.

People just seemed so oblivious, so apathetic. His family was kind of clueless about what he'd been through and how to respond to it and so it was a difficult time for him. He felt himself being pulled into a stereotype, as "Okay, Jim has been to Vietnam – this is how he's going to act. This is how he's feeling. This is the assumption were going to make. He's this and he's not that." He gave himself a chance to start with a clean slate without those stereotypes, those preconceptions, by moving on to Oregon.

He absolutely kept to himself that he had been in the service. There might have been two or three people in the whole State that knew he was an Army veteran. Few knew about his Vietnam experience and that's how he wanted it.[42]

MICHAEL HAYES

When I was 17 in 1971 I decided to join the Army. I knew that the Vietnam War was the defining event of my generation and the historian in me wanted to be an eyewitness to the era. I volunteered for Vietnam but by the time I was deployed, January '72, the Vietnamization process was in full implementation. By the end of that year there were only 24,000 American soldiers in Vietnam down from the high water mark of over a half million in 1968. I was disappointed when I was ordered to report to Germany. I served but I thought it was a bore waiting for an attack by the Soviet Union that never came.

When it was over I went back to Brooklyn and received a friendly and warm reception from family and neighbors. No one, however, was at all interested in where I had been or what I had done except for my little 10 year old brother, Tom, who treated me as if I were a returning hero. Later on two people who learned of my service said, "You're what's wrong with this country." and "No wonder we lost the war (Har-Har)." Aside from that I don't recollect many other comments one way or the other. I was surprised that my time in the service was either generally ignored or simply insulted. I didn't think that I deserved any praise or acknowledgement because I didn't do anything special and was not at all heroic or in any way deserving of accolades. I just didn't understand the American people's attitude towards returning veterans.

"We go westward as into the future, with a spirit of enterprise and adventure."
–Henry David Thoreau

Within a month or two of my return I grew restless and yearned more then ever to be a witness to the era, but feeling as if I were just missing it. I decided to hitchhike across the United States to see what's going on in America and, incidentally, in a hunt for my self. I put some clothes and supplies in a backpack and tied on a sleeping bag and a canteen. As I walked out the front door my brother, Kevin, planted a little American flag on my pack. Tom walked by my side to the corner where I patted him on the head and told him "Goodbye." Leaving my brother I crossed the street, stuck out my thumb and within 5 minutes a car stopped, I got in and rode to an entrance ramp of the Verrazano Narrows Bridge, where I hitched another ride and commenced my trek from the very same spot near Fort Hamilton that began my journey into military service three long years before.

On the first day of my trek I went to Philadelphia and looked up an Army buddy. Ted lived with his parents and I slept on the floor in his father's den. I stayed a day or two and then moved on; Columbus, Ohio; Saint Louis, Missouri; Little Rock, Arkansas; Dallas and El Paso, Texas; Las Cruces, New Mexico; Phoenix and The Grand Canyon, Arizona; San Diego, California. Along the way I slept mostly in parks and in cheap motels.

When people picked me up they would often talk and talk and talk. They would tell all about their personal lives; what they thought about their spouse, their kids, their job and things for which they felt guilty. It reminded me of the Confessional. I thought I must have been like a psychologist or a priest to them, except anonymity was absolutely guaranteed and there was no fee or collection basket, just someone to whom they could open up. Then I would be let out on the side of the road, often in the dark, and they would speed away into oblivion leaving me standing all alone in a cloud of dust. I never saw a single one of them again but they became a part of me forever.

Along the way I met what were popularly known as "Jesus Freaks" who asked me if I "met the Lord today?" and gently attempted to convert me from Catholicism to Protestantism. In addition, I spoke to some people, apparently tied to family and work, who expressed envy at my ability to freely wander the open roads. On one occasion while pausing in a small town an attractive young girl, charmed perhaps with my intrepid behavior, treated me with genuine affection. So much so that I was sorely tempted to stay there but reluctantly opted to move along.

> *"Our truest life is when we are in dreams awake."*
> –Henry David Thoreau

On a few nights I went to sleep in the desert off of the side of the road. Once I awoke suddenly in the wee small hours of the velvety black and solemnly silent, lonely morning. I looked up for a long time and studied the sky. There were more stars fixed above than I had seen in my entire life. I stared and stared until I was among them and I began to think about what the whole war was about. What did it all mean? Everything we did in Vietnam and at home over the era. Was it all just a failed continuation of Manifest Destiny? I visualized the map. America begins on the eastern seaboard and heads westward; the Louisiana Purchase, the Annexation of Texas, the War with Mexico, the Indian Wars and then the Spanish American War brings us all the way to the Philippines and if we were to continue westward from there then Vietnam would be a geographically logical next stop. But this time we overreached.

Maybe if any good was going to come out of all of this we might get Presidents who wouldn't lie to us about events that concern our life and our death and we would know never to get involved in senseless wars again. Then, like babies crying, a band of coyote's yipped, the sun shone its early golden light and I was to my feet, back pack on and on my way.

During my travels nothing even remotely bad ever happened to me. Not once. On the contrary, people frequently offered me friendly advice or food. I guess it was apparent that I wasn't eating very much. Not because I didn't have the money but because it just wasn't a priority at the time. Odd. Not a single policeman ever even stopped me for a moment. I never felt freer in my life, either before or since – have I found the America for which I am searching?

I visited some relatives along the way: Uncle Jim in Little Rock, Aunt Peggy in Las Cruces. I caught up with an old friend from Brooklyn, Sal, in Arizona. It happened that he was getting married that week and he asked me

111

to serve as Best Man. A small group of us went out into the desert and my friend and his teenaged-hippie bride-to-be were joined in holy matrimony. One longhaired, bearded fellow sat high on a rock and played "Something" by George Harrison on an acoustical guitar as the wedding commenced. A self-styled minister in casual attire conducted the ceremony. I hung around for a couple of days and then moved on to the Grand Canyon.

One night while sitting around a campfire with a few young people a girl asked one of the other guys why he was wearing an Army jacket. He said he hadn't been in the service but that he thought girls would find it attractive. She said she did not. I said I had been a soldier but I didn't like people knowing. That was the first time I volunteered to anyone on this trip that I had been in the Army. I was ashamed.

When I arrived in San Diego I visited another Army buddy, Steve, who was living with his older sister. I showed up at his front door as I had everyone else's, unexpectedly. I slept on the porch for five nights in my sleeping bag. Steve was attending a local community college and I went over to the campus with him one morning and waited in the library while he attended a class. Browsing around through the stacks I came across a book that contained every known photograph of Abraham Lincoln that was ever taken and presented in chronological sequence. A light clicked on inside of me. I was mesmerized and thought, "I want to learn more about this man and his times."

After that visit I headed home as fast as possible, anxious to register at a local college. Late one day I was in a remote spot in the desert hitching eastward on the side of the road. The sun was setting and there were no cars approaching from either direction. Then I saw a speck on the horizon and as it drew nearer I could make out a motorcycle heading westward. As the bike approached I discerned the figure of a hippie complete with multi-colored bandana tied around his head, long hair and a Fu Manchu mustache. As he whizzed by he flashed the peace sign and rode off into a kaleidoscopic sunset. I watched until the figure disappeared and all that could be heard was the fast-fading roar of the motorcycle's engine until that too vanished into the dry hot desert air. The sight had caused a shaking in my soul and I thought with a mix of melancholy and sentimentalism, "I just saw the spirit of the '60's riding off into history's book."

On a rainy August night, not long after I returned home, I was going to attend a Grateful Dead concert in Jersey City. The show was delayed due to a heavy downpour and so I stood, thin as a rail and soaking wet, outside of the concert venue beneath an entrance way sheltered from what was now a drizzle. I happened to be standing next to someone holding some fireworks under his arm. Two cops took his fireworks and asked to see his ID. Then one of the officers turned to me and demanded my ID. I pointed, with my right hand, to the stranger that had been standing next to me and I said, "You're wasting your time pal, I don't even know this guy." Before the words were out of my mouth the cop had his left hand around my wrist and punched me in the face below my left eye with his right. Instantly four or five of them seemed to come out of nowhere, faces contorted, and began beating me up with their fists or their blackjacks. Some people who had been standing around quickly ran away while others watched with dumbstruck curiosity. Even after one of the cops yanked out my wallet and threw it on the hood of a car and saw my Veterans Administration ID they continued to pummel me. One guy even punched me right in the mouth while my hands were in metal cuffs and behind my back. I suspect that they hit me with their best shots but I was left with just a fat lip and a couple of bumps on the top of my head to show for all of the unnecessary abuse. I was shoved into the back of a "Paddy Wagon" and taken to a police station where I was fingerprinted, photographed, strip-searched and locked in a cage – or is this America?

The arresting officer typed up a report that claimed I was loitering, not simply waiting for the concert to begin, and that I resisted arrest and that I used all sorts of profanity. None of this was even remotely true. When I was allowed to make a phone call I could see a look of remorse on the faces of two of the cops. They took me to the side and gave me two tickets to the now rescheduled Grateful Dead concert. I used my call to ask my policeman father to rescue me. He drove over quickly and spoke to the desk Sergeant on the side, cop to cop, and they immediately let me go on $50 bond. I was spared having to spend the weekend behind bars. (Thanks Pop.) On Monday morning I reported to court, where the police did not show up to testify. My father arranged to have a lawyer friend of the family speak up for me and the case was dismissed; but not before the judge had stern words of warning, qualifying his comments by adding "If the shoe fits wear it." Nothing was said about the police assault. I don't think I'll ever fully understand why those guys did that to me. Clearly I was not a threat to anyone and it would have only taken one or two of them to safely handcuff me without the administration of a beating. I suspect that they thought it would be fun to punch some young guy around and then brag about their big fight over a couple of beers at the local bar. Or perhaps they were envious.

A few nights later, in Brooklyn, sitting with my father and my brother Kevin in the living room with the TV on, Nixon was about to appear and was expected to announce his resignation. My father ordered, "No comments, Mike." Kevin said, "Don't worry, Mike has a strong sense of history." I thought, "He's right, I do."

Nixon quit. It would be a while until Saigon finally fell but I thought that night marked the conclusion of the Vietnam Era for America. I regretted that I missed it but then realized that after all was said and done I had been a witness to … the end.[43]

Endnotes

1   Jim Slattery, AI, December 2017.

2   William Sims, AI, December 2017.

3   Booth, AI, November 2017.

4   Harrison Smith, "Paul Booth, labor leader and antiwar activist, dies at 74," *Washington Post,* Washington, D.C. January 19, 2018.

5   Booth, AI.

6   SYH, 370.

7   Booth, AI.

8   John Ketwig, AI, November 2017.

9   Virginia "Kiddie" Lane, AI, June 2017.

10   Bill Lane, AI, January 1989.

11   William K. Lane, Jr., "Vietnam Vets Without Hollywood … Without Tears," *Wall Street Journal,* New York, N.Y., July 26, 1988.

12   Bill Lane, AI.

13   William K. Lane, Jr., "Vietnam Vets: Ambushed in Hollywood," *Readers Digest,* December 1988. 118–120.

14   The Holocaust Resource Center Oral History Project, "Dachau Liberator A. Kevin Quinn Interview," www.youtube.com, June 29,1989.

15   Mary Kambic, AI, December 2017.

16   Jose Flores, AI, February 2018.

17   Michael Smar, AI, February 2010 and November 2017.

18   Pat O'Leary, AI, January 2018.

19   Billy X. Jennings, AI, September 2019.

20   Sylvan Fox, "Pickets Circle Columbia; Class Reopening Delayed; 720 Protesters Arraigned." *New York Times,* New York, N.Y. May 1, 1968. 1.

21   Susan Dominus, "Disabled During'68 Columbia Melee, a Former Officer Feels Pain, Not Rage," *New York Times,* New York, N.Y. April 25, 1968. B1.

22   Rudd, AI.

23   UML, 88-89.

24   Rudd, AI.

25   Terence V. Hayes, AI, January 2018.

26   Judy Gumbo, AI, November 2017.

27   Susan Schnall, AI, November 2017.

28   "Mutiny Trial, Ranks of Military Critics Growing," *Independent,* Long Beach, California, March 13, 1969. 22.

29   "Convicted Navy 'Peace' Nurse Makes History," *Press Democrat,* Santa Rosa, California, February 4, 1969. 5.

30   "Court–Martial Sentences Antiwar Nurse to Prison," *Fresno Bee, The Republican,* Fresno,

California, February 4, 1969. 7.

31Schnall, AI.

32   Dean Kahler, AI, October 2017.

33   Peter Davies and The Board of Church Society of the United Methodist Church, *The Truth about Kent State; A Challenge to the American Conscience (New York, N.Y., Doubleday Canada, Ltd., 1973)* 13–14.

34   William A. Gordon, *Four Dead in Ohio (Lake Forest, California, North Ridge Books, 1995)* 89.

35   Kahler, AI.

36   *Remembering Vietnam.* National Archives, Washington, D.C., February 15, 2018. (Henceforth RV)

37   Kahler, AI, March 2019.

38   Denny Myer, AI, October 2017.

39   Jim Connelly, AI, February 2018.

40   E.J. Dionne, Jr., AI, February 2018.

41   Kathleen Gunson, AI, November 2017.

42   Jim Schmidt, AI, November 2017.

43   Michael Hayes, *Author's Recollections.*

LZ EASY

Their Own Words

Chuck Searcy
International Advisor, Project RENEW

I was here, in Vietnam, from June 1967 until June 1968. I was an enlisted man and my MOS was 96B20, which was intelligence analyst. I joined because I was getting drafted and I got scared and thought I might get a better deal and not have to go to Vietnam if I enlisted. I signed up for three years instead of two and went straight to Vietnam.

I grew up in a small town called Thomson, Georgia, but Athens has been my home ever since I went to the University there. When I went in the service I had finished two years of college and I dropped out, which is the reason I got on the radar screen of the draft board. When I left Vietnam in 1968 I was really messed up. I was very angry at the US government, at myself, at the circumstances of the war, and I was confused. I thought the situation was horribly unfair to the Vietnamese people, who never asked for a war here. I had one more year in the army, and I was reassigned to Germany, at US Army Headquarters Europe, which gave me a year to decompress and put things into perspective. I got beyond my anger and got focused. I decided I would return to the University of Georgia and get involved somehow in the antiwar movement. At UGA some vet friends and I started a chapter of Vietnam Veterans Against the War (VVAW).

After the war ended, I thought many times that one day I would go back to Vietnam and I hoped it would be in a time of peace. I had no idea of when or how. Years later, in 1992, an old Army buddy was in town from Atlanta for a convention. We had dinner together and by the end of that dinner we decided we were going back as tourists. The trip was remarkable. I was so astonished by the welcome we experienced and the complete absence of any anger or bitterness on the part of the Vietnamese towards two Americans who were former GI's.

Vietnam was really struggling to recover at that time, still suffering quite a lot not only from the destruction and the devastation of the war but also from an embargo that had been imposed and strangled them economically for twenty years. So during that trip I started thinking I would like to come back and find some way to do something to help. I didn't have any idea what or how. The opportunity came in 1995 with a hospital orthopedic project in Hanoi, sponsored by Vietnam Veterans of America Foundation (VVAF). I agreed to set it up and manage it for three years. More than 20 years later, here I am, still here.

In 2001 I left VVAF and joined the Vietnam Veterans Memorial Fund (VVMF) to start a project partnership with the Provincial Government of Quang Tri (quong-tree), the former DMZ, the temporary border between north and south during the war. Quang Tri officials wanted us to help them deal with the problem of bombs and mines in a comprehensive and integrated way, to take an approach that was strategic. They wanted to try to move toward a real solution to the problem. Up until then a lot of efforts were underway but they were not well coordinated and without a sharp focus of activity.

Previously, Vietnamese army units and civilians were moving around with metal detectors but without the benefit of maps or survey data or more precise information from local people that would help to speed up the process and reduce the cost and try to bring an end to this problem. So that's why Project Renew was begun, at the request of the Vietnamese. It has evolved into a substantial and successful effort to deal with the problem of land mines, cluster munitions, and other unexploded ordnance. Ten years ago we got a lot of help from Norwegian People's Aid (NPA), an international organization that came in as a partner and brought world-class expertise in de-mining and post-conflict response. Along the way we all realized, the Vietnamese, our partners and other colleagues, that the definition of the problem we were using, the goal that everyone was seeking, was not really appropriate. It was not going to work.

Everybody talked about cleaning up every bomb and mine in Vietnam no matter how long it would take or how much it would cost. Even President Clinton acknowledged that during his visit here in 2000. But based on the practical experience of our teams and our staff in Quang Tri, they came to the conclusion that the real goal, the more realistic goal, was not to "clean up every bomb and mine," because that could never be done. The real goal should be to make Quang Tri Province and Vietnam safe. That goal is achievable, and that's what Project Renew has demonstrated over the past fourteen years.

A measure of that success is the accident rate. For more than thirty years there was an average of seventy or eighty accidents a year, from 1975 onward. 2018 was the first year since 1975 that there was not a single accident in Quang Tri Province - no deaths, no injuries, not a single casualty. That's a little bit miraculous, to be truthful. But it has been our goal all along.

Zero accidents, that's the goal. Zero accidents, zero explosions, zero incidents, zero deaths, zero injuries – and we hope to maintain that record every year from now on. There's no guarantee, of course, that there'll never be another accident but the approach now is quite methodical, based on a combination of good local information, maps provided by the US Department of Defense, highly trained and equipped clearance teams, and quick response to call-ins reporting ordnance found.

With thanks to the US government we have very detailed maps of bombing runs planned and executed during the war. Survey data is collected by teams going around from village to village and house to house, they gather information from residents about their experience and that's really the best indicator, because the maps aren't always accurate. A map of a bombing run is not necessarily what pilots actually did, but it's an indicator.

If there's data about cluster munitions strikes, for example, a survey team can go there and they'll find out rather quickly if there are cluster munitions in that area. If they find one or five there might be twenty or fifty more because that's the nature of the cluster munitions strike. So maps and data are good indicators, and combined with what the local people tell the teams, they have a picture that helps pinpoint the ordnance. So teams don't waste a lot of time and effort just wandering around swinging metal detectors. They go to where the indicators are very strong and where they'll likely find ordnance. It's all based on evidence. This is combined with teaching the kids, the villagers, the adults, the farmers, how to identify the ordnance, how to be safe, how to protect themselves by knowing what the ordnance is, and the danger. We challenge them to report the ordnance and we make them understand that it is their responsibility to protect the members of their family and their community. They have to call in when they find explosive ordnance and they do.

And so our Renew-NPA teams and the other teams working in the area like Mines Advisory Group (MAG), Peace Trees, they get calls everyday, starting early, maybe three calls, five calls, eight calls a day. Whatever they are doing elsewhere at that moment, if a call is more urgent than the task they're working on they'll get in the trucks, take the ambulance, and they'll go to that site. After they assess the threat, they'll likely evacuate the area. People may have to leave their homes for two or three hours. The team then destroys the ordnance. They may scout the area and if they find more ordnance, if there's more contamination found, they may send another team back the next day.

Last year there were more than seven hundred calls from people reporting ordnance that they had found, and the result was that the RENEW-NPA teams destroyed more than 7,000 bombs. Since RE-NEW-NPA teams started working in recent years more than 70,000 bombs have been destroyed. Other teams efforts have more than qua-drupled that total. So the effort is working. But the real evidence of suc-cess, the real goal is to keep people safe, and that's a much more use-ful framework that everybody understands. Actually, today I am more hopeful and more confident then I have been in the last twenty years that these issues will be resolved soon and at least we'll be able to bring some "closure" to this issue. Confident that the problem will be solved, not that it'll just go away. Certain that we can address this issue in a way that will bring some relief to families in need of assurance, and some confidence among the population in these areas that they're safe from bombs and mines.

I think we can reach that point relatively soon, within the next five to ten years. And that will be a point where we as veterans, and as Americans, can say that finally, after half a century, we stepped up and did what we should have done forty years ago, and we've helped Vietnam deal with these threats. Vietnam should be able to manage their tragic legacy long into the future, effectively, and at little cost. That should finally offer some measure of satisfaction for us, as Americans, after all these years.[1] https://landmines.org.vn

AL WELLMAN

My disappointment was our Cold War military system and, partic-ularly, the all-volunteer force we have now is really pushing us to-ward any kind of military involvement just to justify their jobs. My per-ception is that we were better off with the draft because the draft was at least exposing people to what was going on and those were people who would tell their neighbors about their observations without worrying about losing their jobs.

Decades after Vietnam I was waiting for a bus to carry me home from my office job. A disheveled homeless man talking loudly to himself approached my bus stop waiting bench. "Hey, I know you!" he said. I tried to appear busy reading my magazine, but he stopped and was obviously looking right at me as he said: "We were in Vietnam together." I looked up and told him I didn't recognize him, so he told me his story. He was exactly my age, and had grown up in rural Oregon. It was the other side of the continent; but his hometown in Oregon, like mine in Maine, was populated by people who earned their living working in the woods and on dairy farms. When I went to college after high school graduation, he enlisted with the rest of his high school football team. They were sent to Vietnam, and he was the only one to come home. Then I recognized him. He was like the boys I grew up with. He was me. But I had been lucky, and he had not.[2]

JIM SLATTERY

I tell you this, in 1990 my son went into the Navy and he was there for the attack on Kuwait. He was in an amphibious assault ship and they were the ones that come in from the sea. He was part of that and I was very proud of him. And I have a grandson looking at the Navy right now and I sure am not gonna talk him out of it. He's 17-18 right in that area. He's looking at diesel mechanic.

WILLIAM L. SIMS

Young people need to understand what war is about. Nobody likes war, period. So when you're going to defend certain things understand what you're doing. I was blessed to go to Vietnam to learn and survive and come back and still work with veterans. I don't regret, you can't. I learned a lot. I also sit on the board of the Center for Veterans Issues. So there's something about giving back.

HEATHER BOOTH

For people who care about building a better and more democratic world, there is often the greatest progress at the moments when there is the greatest danger – IF we organize and take action with others.

The most important lesson for me out of the 1960's and the Vietnam War era is if you organize you can change the world, but you have to organize.

JOHN KETWIG

I'm a bitter Vietnam veteran. God damn them! They took me right out of my life, shaved my head, put me in a green suit and sent me to the other side of the world where people were trying to kill me. I didn't appreciate that and still don't. The truth about Vietnam is very different from what you see on TV and the movies. If a recruiter is ever after you tell him he's a liar.

BILL LANE

Veterans that are homeless or can't hold a job or are somehow messed up blamed the Vietnam experience for messing up their lives. All that stuff is garbage. They're losers and I don't want to be considered one of them.

MARY KAMBIC

Getting arrested was the most rattling experience. You feel creepy all the time for a long time and it didn't go away. Some of my Professors were arrested too but it made a kinship with those people. That was probably good that we stuck together then. That was the biggest thing that happened to me that was negative.

JOSE FLORES

I have friends who died from Agent Orange. Nobody ever educated us about Agent Orange. It was being sprayed outside the base. My friend Tony was 50 years old when he died. He used to spray it from a helicopter. We have a reunion and you ask, "Where's so and so." "Oh, he died from Agent Orange."

But I don't regret a minute. I feel it was my duty. This country has been good to me. I recommend the military for young people and I wish they had the draft because I know a lot of guys who have one foot in the jail and one foot out. I remember when they had the draft the Judge would give them a choice, in a non-violent case, go in the Army or go to jail. Come back in two weeks with the recruiter and I'll let you go.

MICHAEL SMAR

I'm proud of my service. It's given me great comfort. It's given me enormous knowledge of human nature. It allowed me to see people exhibit incredible courage. How many can say that? But it's given me tremendous insight into human nature ... my own nature. It's given me a tremendous breadth of experience that I will never forget. It's made me better. I'm very glad to tell you my story.

PAT O'LEARY

I'm very glad I served because if I didn't I would believe that there's a name on the Vietnam Memorial Wall down there in D.C. that took my place so that would have terrorized me for the rest of my life. I'm glad I served. I'm glad I did what I did.

BILLY X. JENNINGS

The Black Panther Party was noble. You want to talk about the real patriots in America, look at the Party's ten-point program. We changed people's lives. We gave people hope. If you don't have hope in America its all over. We inspired others. We made a difference in people's lives.

History is a weapon. If you want to find out how to change the future you have to step back a couple of steps to find out what happened before you start thinking about what you want to change. If you look back and examine history it will prevent you from falling into a lot of pits that other people had already fallen into before you. That's why we have a website (itsabouttimebpp.com) to educate and organize the people and that's what the Black Panther Party was really all about. We never thought that we were going to go one-on-one with the US government bullet for bullet. We did think that we could educate and organize people. The party was a vanguard organization. All the things that we did are part of the American fiber but we had to struggle to get those things. If you want change you have to struggle. You can't just talk about it – you got to get out there and do it. Create an instrument to organize people just as the Black Panthers did.

MARK RUDD

We made a fundamental mistake of identifying the cops as the enemy and calling them "pigs" and stuff like that. Never dehumanize your opponent. Calling them pigs was a violent act. I think we were wrong in our approach in so many ways because the best strategy is complete and total non-violence. The non-violent antiwar movement worked but where we completely fell down was not keeping at it to gain governmental power. We all went our own way. Whereas the far right stayed in it and now they're in power. They represent just 25% of the population and they're in power! We on the left are not organized for power. It has to be non-violent and it has to be a mass movement. The goal has got to be power.

TERENCE V. HAYES

The press and the empty barrels made the most noises. They wouldn't let the people over in Vietnam conduct the war. They were doing it all from Washington, you know, otherwise it would have turned out a lot better.

As far as those demonstrators we beat up back then, I want them to know that, like they said in the Godfather, "It's nothing personal. It's just business."

JUDY GUMBO

I'm an optimistic person because I see what's going on in terms of what's happened with the women's march, for instance. What's amazing is the whole sexual assault/sexual harassment thing on now. You have, internationally, women standing up against oppressive acts and horrific acts against them/us. So I think that these days social media has really made a difference in terms of communication. I'm looking for more groups to be empowered and so I'm absolutely delighted with what's going on with women, in particular, now.

SUSAN SCHNALL

Today I work with Veterans For Peace and peace and social justice colleagues. Many of the veterans spent time in Southeast Asia in the 1960's and 1970's. A group of us work on the continuing issues of the use of Agent Orange during the war. There is legislation in the House of Representatives aimed to heal the wounds of war by providing care and services to the victims of Agent Orange, clean up of the contaminated land in Vietnam, and care for the children of those originally sprayed by the United States.

DEAN R. KAHLER

I worked for two Attorney's General and The Secretary of State of Ohio. I was an elected County Official. I was also a schoolteacher and I served on many Boards and Commissions to make the community better in some way or another. So I feel I've done more than my fair share of community service and service to my country, over the years.

We must challenge the decisions that the elected officials are making and challenge the values and the mores of our society to make it fair and equitable for everybody. Just look at the equality issues for African Americans and the other people of color, women's rights and the rights of the disabled and the rights of children at this point in time. They still have not been given the full equal rights that the typical white male has. That's why we continue to have the consternation we see in today's society. I mean it's all connected. Even though we've made great strides there are still great strides to be made.

DENNY MEYER

We served in silence – we kept our mouths shut. You never said a word about who you were. You were an invisible man and you had to be vigilant. Of course you never could use the wrong pronoun. You had to say "she" instead of "he" when you were talking about what you did over the weekend and so on. And again you heard discrimination every single day from people you thought were your friends. And if you think that doesn't give you something like PTSD, it does, because you're hyper vigilant. Fortunately, young gay people today who are serving do not have to live like that.

JIM CONNELLY

Of all the things I've done in my life I think Vietnam's probably the thing I feel the most immoral about and that I'm probably ashamed of in a certain way. Some ways I'm proud of it – that I managed to get through the obstacle course, do the things they asked me to do with some kind of professionalism, some kind of degree of sensibility about what I did. But on the other hand I think one of the worst things I did in my life was to go off to a foreign country where nobody had done me any harm and shoot at people that I had no quarrel with.

E.J. DIONNE, JR.

There are a lot of kids out there doing interesting stuff. I see it in my students. There's a lot of awareness that this is a moment for organizing and activism. I think and I hope that they have learned from some of our failures. I think there's a lot of practicality that these kids have about what to do and how to do it that I respect a lot.

KATHLEEN GUNSON

Years past, if you had asked me would I volunteer for nursing service in Vietnam again I would have given you a resounding "NO!" but today, I've found peace with the stumbling blocks life tosses my way, I have gained wisdom for which I am grateful and I have developed many coping skills with which I am blessed. Yes, I would serve again knowing my life would be hell on wheels, forever changed for the good, bad, and the ugly. War is just not nice.

JIM SCHMIDT

I do "truth in recruiting." In a lot of places it's "counter-recruiting" but we try and keep it positive and call it "truth in recruiting." We try to give the kids a more realistic appraisal of the military. What you can expect realistically. You know the recruiters paint a rosy picture and most of what they say is true or mostly true but they certainly don't focus on any of the downsides. So we try to give the kids that. We also serve as advocates. If they want I'll go and talk to a recruiter and ask questions and interpret the contract, and that's part of what I do. It actually helps me to kind of quiet the demons and to atone just a little bit.

MICHAEL HAYES

Recently, when I was in D.C. doing research for this book I awoke early one morning and walked over to the Vietnam Memorial Wall. A hard rain that kept the regular crowds of tourists away had just ended and so I found myself the only one present while standing at the approximate center of the monument. I began to contemplate and then sense the presence of all the men and women who were listed – all 58,000 plus of them. After a few minutes, I noticed the moving reflections of people in the wall's panel and I turned around to see a young family of three. We spoke briefly. They were from South Carolina and they drove up to tour D.C. The mother took a picture of me standing in front of the wall and then the father asked me if I were a war veteran. "No, I wanted to go but I didn't get the chance." Up until that moment I regretted it but then realized that if I had gone I might not be standing there talking to the little family. Sure, I might be fine, like so many thousands of veterans, but on the other hand I might be a name on that wall or one of the seriously wounded, one of the drug addicted, one of the homeless, one of the multitude of suicide victims, one of those who died way too young from Agent Orange exposure or who suffer every night and day with PTSD and have trouble to the present moment even talking about what they saw and what they did. When I interviewed vets for this book they spoke about ghosts more than a few times. One Marine combat veteran wouldn't allow me to interview him because he had "quieted the ghosts" and didn't wish to arouse them.

I remembered that morning in the desert over forty years before, thinking that perhaps we'd learn from Vietnam not to blunder blindly or arrogantly into needless wars. Unfortunately we have. In, unarguably, at least Grenada, Panama and Iraq thus far. Grenada to end American's disapproval of war and what Conservatives termed the "Vietnam Syndrome" and to show that we could still win, particularly if we picked on a small, unsuspecting, lightly armed country. Panama served to really drive the point home and Iraq was out of ignorance, racism, vengeance, arrogance and greed.

Last year I finally went to Vietnam and completed the research for this book. The people were among the kindest, friendliest, humble and polite people I have ever met. I found no bitterness towards Americans whatsoever; in fact it was just the opposite, they love Americans! The Internet and tourists have made it possible for the Vietnamese to see and appreciate our culture; our music, clothing, movies and general style and they appreciate all of it. My Vietnamese friend said that part of the lack of animosity is due to the fact that 65% of the 102 million people are under the age of 44 and therefore could have no first-hand memory of the war.

> *"... if one advances confidently in the direction of his dreams, and endeavors to live the life which he has imagined, he will meet with a success unexpected in common hours."*
>
> – Henry David Thoreau

By now I'm sure you realize that not everything that the people of the Vietnam Era tried to do succeeded. For example, visions of a global revolution never materialized. On the other hand the antiwar movement forced LBJ and then Richard Nixon to engage in negotiations that finally brought about an end to our part in the war. If it were not for the voices of the opposition they would never have been motivated at all to end it. Demonstrators influenced Nixon to stop the draft and, noting the activism of young folks, Congress passed the 27th Amendment lowering the voting age to 18. The spirit of activism in the nation influenced Congress to force Nixon to resign. So activists helped bring about an end to a war, an end to the draft, an amendment to the Constitution and the resignation of a criminal President. Not too bad.

You may wonder, "What does all this have to do with me?" Well if you organize like the Vietnam Era young folks did you can bring about significant changes in our country as well. There are plenty of issues to embrace. Just take a look at the News for ideas; struggle to end war, work to save the environment, demand more gun regulation, fight for affordable health care for everyone, do battle for racial justice. Take your pick – there's plenty that needs to be accomplished. Some of these challenges may seem too difficult or even impossible to realize, but so did the objectives that I listed as having succeeded in the previous paragraph; and they were achieved.

Endnotes

1   Chuck Searcy, AI, March 2018 and March 2019.

2   Al Wellman, AI, November 2017.

3   Nguyen Tran Hieu, AI, March 2018.

4   *The Complete Works of Henry David Thoreau: Canoeing in the Wilderness, Walden, Walking, Civil Disobedience and More,*

AFTERWORD

And so as our chopper sets down on the helipad this part of your journey draws to its conclusion. Thank you for having the intelligence, courage and curiosity to join me. And now, my young friend, it's time to begin another adventure, not into the past this time but rather into the long distant future of the rest of your unique life. Be active, organize and, above all else, please build a better world.

What's Going On?

Mother, mother
There's too many of you crying
Brother, brother, brother
There's far too many of you dying
You know we've got to find a way
To bring some lovin' here today

Father, father
We don't need to escalate
You see, war is not the answer
For only love can conquer hate
You know we've got to find a way
To bring some lovin' here today, oh oh oh

Picket lines and picket signs
Don't punish me with brutality
Talk to me, so you can see
Oh, what's going on
What's going on
Yeah, what's going on
Ah, what's going on

In the mean time
Right on, baby
Right on brother
Right on babe

Father, father, everybody thinks we're wrong
Oh, but who are they to judge us
Simply 'cause our hair is long
Oh, you know we've got to find a way
To bring some understanding here today

Picket lines and picket signs

Don't punish me with brutality
Talk to me
So you can see
What's going on
Ya, what's going on
Tell me what's going on
I'll tell you what's going on
Right on baby
Right on baby

BIBLIOGRAPHY

Addington, Larry H. *America's War in Vietnam: A Short Narrative History.* Bloomington, IN.: Indiana University Press, 2000.

Aguilar-San Juan, Karin (Editor) and **Joyce, Frank** (Editor). *The People Make the Peace: Lessons from the Vietnam War Antiwar Movement.* Charlottesville, VA.: Just World Books, 2015.

Andreas, Joel. *Addicted to War: Why the US Can't Kick Militarism.* Chico, CA.: AK Press, 2015.

Albert, Stew. *Who the Hell is Stew Albert?* Los Angeles, CA.: Red Hen Press, 2004.

Bloom, Joshua and **Martin, Waldo E., Jr.** *Black against Empire: The History and Politics of the Black Panther Party.* Oakland, CA.: University of California Press, 2013.

Bristol, Douglas W., Jr. (Editor) and **Stur, Heather Marie** (Editor). *Integrating the US Military: Race, Gender, and Sexual Orientation since World War II.* Baltimore, MD.: Johns Hopkins University Press, 2017.

Collins, Gail. *When Everything Changed: The Amazing Journey of American Women From 1960 to the Present.* New York, N.Y.: Little, Brown and Company, 2009.

Commission for Research on the Party History. *Ho Chi Minh's Life and Cause.* Hanoi, Vietnam: The Gioi Publishers, 2016.

Davies, Peter. *The Truth About Kent State: A Challenge to the American Conscience.* New York, N.Y.: Farrar Straus and Giroux, 1973.

Dallek, Robert. *Lyndon B. Johnson: Portrait of a President.* New York, N.Y.: Oxford University Press, 2004.

Duc, Tran Hong and **Thu, Ha Van.** *A Brief Chronology of Vietnamese History.* Hanoi, Vietnam: The Gioi Publishers, 2014.

Doyle, William. *PT 109: An American Epic of War, Survival, and the Destiny of John F. Kennedy.* New York, N.Y.: Harper Collins, 2015.

Farrell, John A. *Richard Nixon: The Life.* New York, N.Y.: Doubleday, 2017.

Fisher, James T. *Dr. America: The Lives of Thomas A. Dooley 1927–1961.* Amherst, MA.: The University of Massachusetts Press, 1997.

Frank, Nathaniel. *Unfriendly Fire: How the Gay Ban Undermines the Military and Weakens America.* New York, N.Y.: Thomas Dunne Books, 2009.

Freedman, Russell. *Vietnam: A History of the War.* New York, N.Y.: Holiday House, 2016.

Fulsom, Don. *Nixon's Darkest Secrets: The Inside Story of America's Most Troubled President.* New York, N.Y.: Thomas Dunne Books, 2012.

Gates, Henry Louis, Jr. *Life Upon These Shores: Looking at African American History 1513 – 2008.* New York, N.Y.: Alfred A, Knopf, 2013.

Goldman Ruben, Susan. *Freedom Summer: The 1964 Struggle for Civil Rights in Mississippi.* New York, N.Y.: Holiday House, 2014.

Gordon, William A. *Four Dead in Ohio: Was There a Conspiracy at Kent State?* Laguna Hills, CA.: North Ridge Books, 1995.

Goscha, Christopher. *Vietnam: A New History.* New York, N.Y.: Basic Books, 2016.

Green, Sam and **Siegal, Bill.** The Weather Underground, Documentary, 2002.

Hastings, Max. *Vietnam: An Epic Tragedy, 1945-1975.* New York, N.Y.: Harper, 2018.

Hayden, Tom. *Hell No: The Forgotten Power of the Vietnam Peace Movement.* New Haven, CT.: Yale University Press, 2017.

Holzer, Henry and **Erika.** *"Aid and Comfort": Jane Fonda in North Vietnam.* Jefferson, N.C.: McFarland and Company, Inc., Publishers, 2002.

Kerry, John. *Every Day Is Extra.* New York, N.Y.: Simon and Schuster, 2018.

Ketwig, John. *...And A Hard Rain Fell: A GI's True Story of the War in Vietnam.* New York, N.Y.: Sourcebooks, 20th Anniversary Edition, 2008.

---. *Vietnam Reconsidered: The War, the Times and Why They Matter.* Waterville, OR.: Trine Day LLC, 2019.

Kovic, Ron. *Born on the Fourth of July.* Brooklyn, N.Y.: Akashic Books, Anniversary edition, 2016.

Lembcke, Jerry. *Hanoi Jane: War, Sex and Fantasies of Betrayal.* Amherst and Boston, MA.: University of Massachusetts Press, 2010.

Logevall, Fredrik. *Embers of War: The Fall of an Empire and the Making of America's Vietnam.* New York, N.Y.: Random House Trade Paperbacks, 2012.

Marlantes, Karl. *Matterhorn.* New York, N.Y.: Grove Press, 2011.

Matthews, Chris. *Jack Kennedy: Elusive Hero.* New York, N.Y.: Simon and Schuster, 2011.

McMaster, H.R. *Dereliction of Duty.* New York, N.Y.: Harper Collins Publishers, 1997.

McNamara, Robert S. and **Van Demark, Brian.** *In Retrospect: The Tragedy and Lessons of Vietnam.* New York, N.Y.: Vintage Books, 1995.

New York Historical Society Museum and Library. *1945-1975 The Vietnam War.* London, England: D. Giles Limited, 2017.

Moore, Hal G. and **Galloway, Joseph L.** *We Were Soldiers Once and Young.* New York, N.Y.: Random House Publishing Group, 1992.

O'Brien, Tim. *The Things They Carried.* New York, N.Y.: Mariner Books, 2009.

Parrish, John A. *Autopsy of War.* New York, N.Y.: Thomas Dunne Books, 2012.

Pekar, Harvey. *Students for a Democratic Society: A Graphic History.* New York, N.Y.: Hill and Wang, 2009.

Perritano, John. *John McCain: An American Hero.* New York, N.Y.: Sterling Children's Books, 2018.

Rudd, Mark. *My Life with SDS and the Weathermen Underground.* New York, N.Y.: Harper Collins Publishers, 2009.

Satin, Mark. *Manual for Draft-Age Immigrants to Canada.* Toronto, CA.: House of Annasi, 1968.

Schmitz, David F. *Richard Nixon and the Vietnam War: The End of the American Century.* Lanham, MD.: Rowman and Littlefield, 2016.

Schoendoerffer, Pierre. *The Anderson Platoon. A Documentary Film.* French Broadcasting System, 1967.

Sheehan, Neil. *The Pentagon Papers: The Secret History of the Vietnam War.* New York, N.Y.: Racehorse Publishing, 2017.

Shilts, Randy. *Conduct Unbecoming: Gays and Lesbians in the US Military, Vietnam to the Persian Gulf.* New York, N.Y.: Saint Martin's Press, 1993.

Terry, Wallace. *Bloods.* New York, N.Y.: Ballantine Books, 1984.

Thomas, Pat and **Rubin, Jerry.** *DiD iT! From Yippie to Yuppie, An American Revolutionary.* Seattle, WA.: Fantagraphics, 2017.

Vien, Nguyen Khac. *Vietnam a Long History.* Hanoi, Vietnam: The Gioi Publishers, 2015.

Ward, Geoffrey C. and **Burns, Ken.** *The Vietnam War: An Intimate History.* New York, N.Y.: Alfred A. Knopf, 2017.

Widmer, Ted. *Listening In: The Secret White House Recordings of John F. Kennedy.* New York, N.Y.: Hyperion Books, 2012.

Zinn, Howard. *A People's History of the United States.* New York, N.Y.: Harper and Row, 1980.

AUTHOR'S INTERVIEWS – Daniel Berrigan, SJ, Heather Booth, Hugh Boyle, Ph.D., McGeorge Bundy, Jim Connelly, E.J. Dionne, Jr., Ph.D., Jose Flores, Judy Gumbo, Ph.D., Kathleen Gunson, RN, Terence V. Hayes, Nguyen Tran Hieu, Billy X. Jennings, Dean Kahler, Mary Kambic, John Ketwig, Bill Lane, Fredrik Logevall, Ph.D., Denny Meyer, Pat O'Leary, Mark Rudd, Jim Schmidt, Susan Schnall, RN, Chuck Searcy, William Sims, Jim Slattery, Michael Smar, M.D., Perry Watkins and Al Wellman.

PHOTOGRAPH CREDITS – Susan Schnall from estuarypress.com; John Ketwig from www.johnketwig.com; Bill Lane contributed by Terence V. Hayes.; Paul Booth contributed by Heather Booth.; Judy Gumbo from www.yippiegirl.com; Chuck Searcy from Project Renew   landmines.org.vn; Billy X. Jennings and Huey Newton from itsaboutimebpp.com. All other photographs contributed by the interviewees or public domain.

ACKNOWLEDGMENTS

I wish to thank the following people and organizations for their encouragement, support, insights and inspiration: Laurie Austin of the John F Kennedy Presidential Library, Randy Azelton, Jack Bergen of GALA Notre Dame and St. Mary's, Ed Bishop, Dr. Mark Boyle, The Black Panther Party Alumni, Sabine Dabady, Disabled American Veterans, Richard Genest, John Hughes, Dakota Jablon and Andrew Patrick of The Coalition to Stop Gun Violence, Uncle Dan Kelleher, Virginia "Kiddie" Lane, Dorothy Lazard of the Oakland Public Library History Room, Rosemary Luzzi of ALTOUR, Kris Millegan of TrineDay Publishing, The National Archives in Washington, D.C., The New-York Historical Society, Kevin O'Connor of Charlotte Sheedy Literary Agency, Louise Polizzotto, Sal and Aaron Porrazzo of Desert Digital Imaging, Glen Ross and NABVETs, Vietnam Veterans of America, Marty Webster and Vietnam Veterans Against the War, War Museum in Ho Chi Minh City, Dana Wyles and The Zinn Education Project.

Index

Michael Hayes earned a Master's Degree in American History and has taught US History as an Adjunct Professor at the State University of New York. He is the author of *Oak Hill: Voices from an American Hamlet: An Oral History* and *Jimmy Carter: With Family, Friends and Foes*. He has contributed to *The Long Island Historical Journal* as well as *Modern American Environmentalists,* a biographical encyclopedia. In addition, Mike has been a long-time high school social studies teacher.